CONTENTS

Library of Congress Cataloging-in-Publication Data is available.
ISBN: 978-1-68247-983-4 (print)
ISBN: 978-1-68247-992-6 (eBook)

Only America
has such an Airplane

When the United States Navy ordered hundreds of these Vought shipboard fighters, American aviation took another great stride forward. For the first time on either side of the Atlantic, here is an airplane that meets the highly specialized requirements of shipboard use and still produces the blazing speed to match any airplane in the sky. *Only America has such an airplane.*

Until recently, no engine in the world could have supplied the power to make this airplane possible. Now, with the new 2,000-horsepower Pratt & Whitney Double Wasp, Vought engineers have capitalized the opportunities offered by America's far-reaching development of the air-cooled engine.

UNITED AIRCRAFT CORPORATION

EAST HARTFORD · CONNECTICUT

PRATT & WHITNEY ENGINES | VOUGHT-SIKORSKY AIRPLANES | HAMILTON STANDARD PROPELLERS

INTRODUCTION

RARELY IS AN AIRCRAFT DESIGN SO INSPIRED that it elicits near-universal recognition and acclaim. With Vought Corsairs in active-duty squadrons for more than 50 years, one Corsair model, the F4U, stands alone. The plane's designation denotes the fourth in the fighter series produced by Vought, given the suffix *U* to conform to the Navy naming convention that applied a letter to indicate the manufacturer—with Vought's airplanes always ending in U. In more than 110 years of naval aviation history, only a few Navy aircraft have been acknowledged as game-changers that singularly tipped the balance in air warfare. The Vought F4U Corsair heads a short list of such aircraft by dint of its supremely efficient lines—a melding of the highly developed Double Wasp power plant, the outsized Hydromatic propeller that it drove, and the finely tuned airframe that wrapped it. Navy and Marine Corps aviators held the Corsair in high esteem for its ruggedness, speed, and adaptability as a fighter and bomber, long after its first appearance in the South Pacific in World War II through the closing weeks of the Korean War. The Corsair's potency made it sought after by allied air forces long after its final days in the U.S. inventory, rendering vital service in French livery at Dien Bien Phu, and finally, with South American air forces in the so-called Soccer War of the late 1960s.

In early flight trials, the experimental prototype Corsair, the XF4U-1, turned heads and fanned enthusiasm with Naval and Army aviators alike when on 1 October 1940 it flew at an astounding 405 mph. Among U.S. fighter designs of the prewar years, only the Lockheed twin-engine P-38 had topped the 400 mph mark. Major General Henry "Hap" Arnold, then chief of the Army Air Forces and an avid proponent of the P-38, expressed an interest in the XF4U-1 and its power plant that went beyond mere curiosity. Previously, he had looked askance at Pratt & Whitney's pursuit of large radial engine development as a misplaced investment priority. He admonished the company to focus on coaxing more performance out of the turbocharged liquid-cooled inline engine. Allison Engine Company already produced the industry-leading 12-cylinder V-1710, and a new production source might spur Allison to shave costs and streamline output. Now, with proof at hand of the Corsair's explosive speed, he urged Pratt & Whitney to discontinue liquid-cooling development and press forward on radial development.[1] The Navy soon weighed in. Rear Admiral John Towers, then chief of the Bureau of Aeronautics, observed the record-

With aircraft orders numbering in the hundreds, and to underscore the Corsair's American pedigree for British Commonwealth buyers, Vought began an aggressive product advertising campaign in 1941 with dynamic posters. The advertisement copy underscores the synergy brought to bear in the Corsair through Vought's collaboration with other subsidiaries of United Aircraft, namely Pratt & Whitney engines and Hamilton Standard propellers. (Vought Aircraft Company Collection, University of Texas at Dallas)

setting speed run and proclaimed the XF4U-1 to be the "fastest fighter in the world."[2]

The Vought Company and the Navy confronted their share of development delays with the Corsair, which was endearingly labeled "Hose Nose," "U-Bird," or, simply, "Hog." The plane's unforgiving tendencies on carrier flight decks soured opinions and nearly ruined its reputation. But Vought would not let those gripes scuttle the introduction of an extraordinary combat aircraft. With the encouragement of many in uniform who had become early advocates—some of whom had flown it in combat—Vought rectified the issues, permitting the Corsair to earn its place in the pantheon of war-winning, historic naval aircraft.

The scoreboard at the end of World War II showed 2,140 shootdowns of enemy aircraft, with the loss of only 189 Corsairs in combat—a ratio of better than 11:1. Breaking down those statistics further, Navy and Marine Corps Corsair pilots managed a still respectable 8.8:1 ratio against Japanese fighter-type aircraft in aerial combat. That compares to the F6F Hellcat's impressive 13.8:1 ratio in aerial combat against fighter aircraft. Here, one might pause to remember that carrier-based Hellcats had a much richer target pool all to themselves in 1944 when Corsairs had yet to be assigned to carriers. Yet, for the entire war, the Corsair—in its shorter time aboard carriers—delivered 2.5 times the bomb tonnage as the Hellcat, again foreshadowing the F4U's utility as a fighter-bomber.[3]

When surveying the record of published histories of the Corsair, what is immediately apparent is that the subject has been well documented. None of those histories can match the authenticity of Boone Guyton's *Whistling Death*, a firsthand account of test-flying the Corsair, with the possible exception of *The Jolly Rogers*, Tom Blackburn's firsthand account of flying the Corsair in combat. One of the earliest and most comprehensive treatments is *Corsair* by historian Barrett Tillman, truly the dean of naval aviation historians. Tillman's narrative brings forth the many personal stories of pilots who flew the airplane while detailing steps in the Corsair's development and, importantly, its acceptance in the fleet. Two more recent publications complement the growing library of Corsair histories. Martin Bowman has rendered an exceptionally strong history in *The Men Who Flew the Vought F4U Corsair*, with greater attention devoted to the experience of the Fleet Air Arm in World War II. James D'Angina added to the growing record with *Vought F4U Corsair*, citing voluminous detail with production numbers and configuration specifics. The most comprehensive look at Corsairs in the Korean War is Warren Thompson's *Naval Aviation in the Korean War*. At the other end of the spectrum, apart from a purely narrative style, Bert Kinzey has printed an excellent photographic record of F4U in part-by-part detail over two volumes that have been well received by the scale modeling community. All of these excellent publications were sourced for the story that follows.

This work differs in finding a middle path between an anthology of personal combat vignettes and a detailed photo compilation appreciated so much by scale modelers. Where personal stories are presented, they are used to reveal some unique trait or characteristic of the F4U. The emphasis that readers should find new here is a deeper look at the origin story for the Corsair, an examination of the competitive, contractual, and manufacturing beginnings of the program and a more

cohesive chronology of the carrier suitability issues and their resolution. Here, too, the Corsair is compared with other aircraft, in performance measures more relevant to aerial combat that fighter pilots would recognize and appreciate.

An overriding interest in Corsair history was imprinted on me through years of employment with the LTV Corporation, a company whose identity traced directly through the Chance Vought Company to its forerunner, the Vought-Sikorsky Company, original maker of the F4U Corsair. In my time with LTV, fellow employees still used Vought as the preferred common name for their company. The Navy was phasing out its last Corsair, the A-7, from active service then. Nevertheless, the company seized an opportunity to draw out new capability from its utilitarian airframe by adding new avionics and an afterburning engine for the Air National Guard. Budget cuts spelled the end of that upgrade in the Air Guard, and with it the end of the Corsair line. But in my time at Vought, there was a palpable sense of history that every employee shared and recognized in one another—that they were part of a tradition of innovation in aircraft design, meticulously exquisite engineering, and abiding product support to the Navy and Marine user that lived on—a tradition defined in the creation of the F4U and vouchsafed by the airplane's phenomenally successful wartime reputation.

My gratitude is extended to many who assisted me in large measure or small, beginning with Jack Russell and Tom Cutler at Naval Institute Press. Illustrators Bertrand Brown, Dave Douglass, and Chris Busbridge produced very impressive, highly detailed images of Corsairs, Hellcats, and Zekes. Thanks to Roy Sutherland of Barracuda Studios for his assistance; to Bert Kinzey for Corsair line drawings; and to Tommy Thomason for permission to use photographs and research on the XF4U-1. Thanks go to Patrizia Nava, archivist for Vought company records at the University of Texas at Dallas, and to Alicia Henneberry Ralph and Sarah Bseirani at the National Archives and Records Administration's still photo branch and text reference branch, respectively, as well to Alyson Mazzone at the U.S. Marine Corps history division. Sincere thanks also go to Russ Lee, Brian Nicklas, and Elizabeth Borjas at the National Air and Space Museum reference desk, as well as to Danielle Swanson in collections and Jessica Williams, head curator of the Intrepid Museum. I am greatly appreciative of the graphics wizardry of Aldo Spadoni, who rendered helpful illustrations.

The official history of the F4U began in 1938 with the Bureau of Aeronautics solicitation. It really began more than two decades before, when the company was founded by Chauncey (Chance) Vought, and invigorated in the early 1930s by a succession of gifted aeronautical designers. This story of the F4U begins there.

NOTES

1. Martin W. Bowman, *The Men Who Flew the Vought F4U Corsair* (Barnsley, UK: Pen & Sword Books, 2021), 6.

2. Clark G. Reynolds, *Admiral John Towers* (Annapolis, MD: Naval Institute Press, 1991), 335.

3. Stuart B. Barber, *Naval Aviation Combat Statistics World War II*, OPNAV-P- 23V No. A129 (Washington, DC: Air Branch, Office of Naval Intelligence, Office of the Chief of Naval Operations, 17 June 1946), 14, 42.

CORSAIR PROVENANCE

Beginning in 1925, the air-cooled engine began to assert itself in the scheme of things. Chance Vought was one of the first to appreciate its possibilities. He knew that if an engine of this type could be developed in dependability, it had outstanding advantages. This was particularly true in the field of naval work because of the possibilities of reducing weight and size, which were vital in naval aviation.

—E. E. Wilson, president, United Aircraft, January 1931[1]

FOUNDING A LEGACY

Throughout naval aviation's first decade, the dominant aircraft supplier was the Curtiss Aeroplane and Motor Company. As naval aircraft became more specialized and numbers increased steadily after World War I, other companies were added to the roster of notable producers. Among them was the Chance Vought Corporation. Appreciating the Corsair's legacy requires a deeper look into the company and personalities that spawned it.

The founder, Chauncey "Chance" Vought, was only 13 years old when the Wright Brothers' Flyer lifted off from Kitty Hawk, North Carolina. That event ignited an intense interest in aeronautics when press coverage leaked out. At 19, Vought was a draftsman lofting frame members for the McCormack-Romme Cycloplane, commonly called the umbrella plane, an attempt by several eager sponsors to circumvent the Wrights' patent stranglehold on flight control design. The circular-shaped, camberless umbrella achieved successful controlled flights in 1910 but in Vought's view was a freakish and impractical concept, and it never progressed to the point of commercial viability. By his mid-20s, he had catapulted himself to chief engineer of the Wright Company in Dayton, Ohio. U.S. entry into World War I was the catalyst for rapidly expanding market opportunities for experienced designers, and Chance Vought jumped in by founding his own company. With financial backing from sportsman Birdseye Lewis, Vought took a subsidiary role as chief engineer in the new Lewis and Vought Company.

The Vought Company registered a strong start with the design of the VE-7 Bluebird, a standout for simplicity and stability. At a moment when the inventory of naval aircraft was still defined by flying boats and floatplanes, the Bluebird became the first wheeled naval aircraft to take off from an aircraft carrier, the USS *Langley* (CV-1), in 1922. Success with the Bluebird and Lewis' untimely passing in a plane crash in France moved Vought to reorganize as the Chance Vought Corporation. The Bluebird's achievement with the Navy began a run of highly successful Vought aircraft designed for operation from aircraft carriers that was nearly uninterrupted for the next 40 years. And it placed Vought in the company of a handful of other aircraft producers that were held in high regard by the Navy's Bureau of Aeronautics (BuAer), then the Bureau of Naval Weapons, and finally the Naval Air Systems Command for their understanding of the peculiarities of naval aircraft design.

Company founder and visionary designer of early naval aircraft, Chance Vought was the aviation industry pioneer who defined a legacy of engineering and innovation excellence. (Vought Aircraft Company Collection, University of Texas at Dallas)

Indispensable to the Corsair story is the very cordial friendship Vought nurtured with Pratt & Whitney engine company founder Frederick Rentschler, which began during their overlapping tenures at the Wright Company. As a naval officer during World War I, the Princeton-schooled engineering graduate and first-generation American had been detailed to the Wright board as liaison between the service and the manufacturer. In the postwar drawdown, Rentschler—by then resigned from active duty—rose quickly to head the Wright Company. But he found greater opportunity to align his own interests with the Navy's leanings toward bigger engines, especially radial engines, when in 1924 he left Wright to form Pratt & Whitney. With much of his core engineering talent poached from Wright, Rentschler set about to assemble a new, more powerful radial for the Navy that would be the platform for future engine growth. In this work, the Vought-Rentschler relationship would prove fortuitous for both men.

The great debate in the mid-1920s in the aeronautics domain centered on liquid- versus air-cooled engines. From his prior Navy service, Rentschler had grown sensitive to the Navy's push to reduce size, weight, and complexity of aircraft engines, especially for carrier operations. Rentschler understood that radial engines satisfied all these needs. Unlike liquid-cooled engines, they did not rely on a complex arrangement of heavy radiators, tankage, pumps, and piping for cooling fluid. And they could take the pounding that came with repeated landings on a carrier deck "without cracking brazed joints in radiators—since there was no radiator—and springing leaks. Radials weighed less, provided faster climb rates, and simplified maintenance."[2]

THE FIRST CORSAIR

As Pratt & Whitney's president, Rentschler was in a commanding position to promote the Navy's move to an all-radial engine inventory. Chance Vought, through his own contacts inside the Navy, implored BuAer to

The O2U was the first Corsair and the first service airplane designed around the new Pratt & Whitney Wasp air-cooled engine. The Navy typically employed it with floats from ships, while the Marine Corps used it ashore. (Vought Aircraft Company Collection, University of Texas at Dallas)

consider an all-new engine that could deliver at least 350 hp and weigh no more than 650 pounds—specifications that were not then available with any liquid-cooled engine and could only be satisfied with a new radial design. The BuAer engine specialists were willing to offer an enticement: a successful power plant demonstration that met those thresholds would earn Pratt & Whitney a down payment of $90,000 for six engines placed on the loading dock.[3]

With encouragement from Rear Admiral William Moffett, then BuAer chief, and with Chance Vought's prodding, Pratt & Whitney engineered the single-row, nine-cylinder R-1340 Wasp engine. The Secretary of the Navy proclaimed; "A number of new airplanes for shipboard use are being built around this engine. . . . There is every assurance that, as a result of this development, the fleet will soon have aircraft whose performance is far in excess of anything available elsewhere."[4]

Vought's company was already working on a new aircraft design built around a generic class of radials. The new Wasp neatly fit the Vought design. The Navy agreed and ordered two Wasp-powered prototypes in 1927, designating them XO2U-1s. The popular name for the production O2U suggested by Vought and adopted by the Navy was Corsair. The Corsair was a spectacularly successful program for Vought, and the aircraft proved a reliable and versatile workhorse for the Navy and Marines in observation or scouting squadrons attached to the early aircraft carriers, battleships, and cruisers. The Marine Corps used O2Us to good effect operating with squadrons ashore. When operating at sea with the battleships and cruisers, floats were worn for water landing and recovery. On the carriers, the Corsairs could operate with floats or conventional wheeled landing gear. With international users included, production ran to 378 aircraft. Thus began a Corsair lineage, exemplified by airframe designs superbly harmonized to the greater engine output coming from Pratt & Whitney, satisfying a multiplicity of Navy and Marine warfighting needs. One of the more conspicuous service episodes that directly involved the O2U Corsair and underscored its utility occurred in 1928 in Nicaragua. A U.S. Marine infantry patrol was ambushed and cut off from reinforcements and ammunition replenishment by Sandino rebels. Marine aviator First Lieutenant Christian Schilt was in country but based miles away with Observation Squadron VO-7M. Schilt volunteered for a very challenging resupply flight in his Vought O2U. One flight soon became 10 flights over 3 days into unprepared landing strips to bring in urgently needed medical supplies and a new ground commander and to bring out 18 wounded Marines. Schilt's personal bravery was recognized with the Medal of Honor. By extension, Vought was building a reputation throughout Marine Corps aviation for rugged, stable aircraft.

By 1928 Vought Corporation's preeminence in the military aircraft manufacturing business—especially with the Navy and Marine Corps—was assured, perhaps surpassed only by Boeing. Manufacturing space at Long Island City, New York, was inadequate to the need for floor space for O2U assembly and for anticipated follow-on programs. By the end of that year, Vought began construction on a new plant in East Hartford, Connecticut. Early the next year, the Vought Corporation voluntarily joined a consortium of aerospace businesses under the umbrella of United Aircraft and Transport Corporation. With this amalgamation of airframe and engine manufacturers and airline companies, the founders Bill Boeing, Fred Rentschler, and Chance Vought intended to expand market share by vertically integrating the necessary elements of airplane construction and commercial air service. The net benefit for the Vought Corporation was to bring the company into closer physical proximity and business collaboration with the favored engine provider, Pratt & Whitney, and propeller supplier, Hamilton Standard. Chance Vought would not live to see the hoped-for synergy from the alliance, passing from septicemia in mid-1930.

THE SECOND CORSAIR

During the earliest days of the United Aircraft holding company, Vought's O2U evolved further, mainly through incorporation of a new Pratt & Whitney R-1690 Hornet engine adding 30 percent more horsepower, along with strengthened frames and longerons. Differences from the first O2U were significant enough to warrant a designation change to O3U, but the Corsair name was retained.

Barely two years after the introduction of the O3U, Pratt & Whitney had progressed to the R-1535 Twin Wasp Junior, a 2-row, 14-cylinder radial developing nearly twice the horsepower of the R-1340 in the O2U. To stay apace, BuAer asked industry for all-metal, two-seat fighter designs mated to the newest Pratt & Whitney engine. Vought complied, but the Navy changed its thinking on two-seat fighters and asked for a scout bomber built around the engine. Vought abandoned its first prototype and built a second—the XSBU-1—with beefed-up structure to tolerate the rigors of dive-bombing, still mated to the new Twin Wasp Junior. The XSBU design benefited from the arrival of Rex Beisel as assistant chief engineer. When Beisel was appointed lead designer of the XSBU, his penchant for lean airframe design and his exacting approach to engine integration and drag reduction ensured that maximum energy could be extracted from the power plant. He tailored the airframe to serve the engine, to offer as little airstream resistance as possible, and to exploit industry innovations that could aid in that effort. As a result, the XSBU-1 borrowed many of the features introduced with the O3U, including the new National Advisory Committee for Aeronautics cowl, adjustable cowling gills, canopied cockpit, and controllable pitch propeller.

Marine Lieutenant Christian F. Schilt, in front of a Vought O2U, flew the plane under fire in Nicaragua in 1927 to evacuate wounded Marines. For his courageous flights, he was awarded the Medal of Honor. (Vought Aircraft Company Collection, University of Texas at Dallas)

The Navy was impressed and selected the SBU over seven other industry competitors to become its standard carrier-based dive-bomber. The SBU became the second Vought aircraft to bear the name Corsair, and Rex Beisel was the acknowledged force behind its creation. His talent would soon prove indispensable to creation of the next Corsair, the F4U. Meanwhile, the SBU served in bombing squadrons in *Saratoga*, *Lexington*, and *Ranger* until 1940 when, due to the rapid turnover of carrier aircraft types, most were retired to take up new employment as bombing trainers at Pensacola.

When the reworked prototype XSBU-1 was delivered to Anacostia Naval Air Station in Washington, DC, for Navy tests in 1934, company leaders were momentarily distracted by tectonic shifts in the aircraft industry. Corporate relationships were altered in ways that profoundly affected Vought—ultimately, as it turned out, in a quite beneficial way. The holding company to which the Vought Corporation subscribed would not last beyond 1934 in its original configuration. That year, the U.S. government determined that large holding companies were anti-competitive and decreed that the United Aircraft holding company had to be split into three wholly separate groups: manufacturers west of the Mississippi to be merged with Boeing, the commercial passenger businesses consolidated as United Air Lines, and those companies east of the Mississippi (Vought, Hamilton Standard Propellers, Sikorsky, and Pratt & Whitney Engines) merged as United Aircraft Company. Fred Rentschler was installed as the head of

Rex Beisel—Vought Chief Engineer and Designer

The son of a coal miner, Rex Beisel was born into meager circumstances. As a child, he lived in a tent near his father's work in Cumberland, Washington.

Rex Beisel, Vought's chief engineer in 1938, is credited with leading the development of the bent-wing Corsair, an ingenious and efficient design that combined the most powerful engine available with the largest diameter propeller ever built. (Vought Aircraft Company Collection, University of Texas at Dallas)

When not in school, he worked as a rail-splitter, a surveyor's helper, and finally as a breaker boy in the same coal mine as his father, earning $2.60 a day to pay his way through the engineering program at the University of Washington.

Beisel's high marks on the civil service exam in engineering garnered immediate attention and a job offer from the Navy's Bureau of Aeronautics as a draftsman, despite him having ailments that would have stymied most: He was deaf in one ear, color-blind, had no sense of smell, and suffered from early onset Parkinson's disease. For his work on the NC flying boats, he was personally commended by bureau chief Rear Admiral William A. Moffet.

Beisel struck out for private employment with the Curtiss Aeroplane and Motor Corporation, where he oversaw design of the R2C-1, a racer flown by Navy Lieutenant Al Williams to capture the 1923 Pulitzer trophy in the National Air Races. Joining Vought in 1931, he was immediately appointed lead designer of a new Navy dive bomber, the SBU. A technical paper describing the SBU's groundbreaking cowl design garnered him and his coauthors the Wright Brothers Medal in 1934.

Promoted to chief engineer, he oversaw the creation of the OS2U Kingfisher floatplane in 1937. Beisel possessed the imagination, persuasive skill, and technical credentials that placed him in the right position at the right moment to lead the creation of a new Navy carrier-based fighter, one to be built around the new Pratt and Whitney R-2800 engine.

The second Corsair, the SBU, was the first of its type to exceed 200 mph. Rex Beisel's unique talent as design team leader for the SBU became apparent, with the airplane benefiting from the optimum combination of airframe and the new Pratt & Whitney Twin Wasp engine. (Vought Aircraft Company Collection, University of Texas at Dallas)

United Aircraft, with Vought retaining its status as a stand-alone subsidiary.

A key leadership change for Vought in the years immediately following was appointment of C. J. McCarthy as general manager. Massachusetts Institute of Technology graduate McCarthy's aeronautical engineering expertise ran deep from his years of work as a draftsman and structures design leader for the Navy's Bureau of Construction and Repair. There, he did the strength calculations for the Curtiss NC flying boats, one of which, the NC-4, became the first aircraft to cross the Atlantic in 1919. That success propelled McCarthy to appointment as deputy chief of the Bureau of Weapons, where he oversaw structures for all Navy aircraft acquisitions. From government service to private employment at Vought, the one constant on display was his ability to manage a large technical enterprise, vital to the company's positioning to respond to a new fighter solicitation from the Navy in 1938. Under McCarthy's tutelage, F4U Corsair designers Beisel and his understudy, Russ Clark, benefited mightily by the encouragement, ample resources, and expertise that were freely offered.

Any preoccupation with the industry shake-up of 1934 did not last beyond Vought's move to East Hartford. The Chance Vought Company was first and foremost consumed by advancing aircraft design. McCarthy nudged Vought designers to produce their first two monoplanes, a prototype scout-bomber, the XSB2U-1 Vindicator, and the XOS2U-1 Kingfisher scout plane. Finally, with Vought and Pratt & Whitney so closely situated, the appearance of conflict forced the Vought Corporation make its last prewar move away from Pratt & Whitney to Stratford, Connecticut, where it briefly cohabited with Sikorsky to form Vought-Sikorsky. As the move got underway, plans were already on the boards for a new revolutionary monoplane fighter optimized for speed, a fighter that would become the third—and most consequential design—to bear the name Corsair.

NOTES

1. E. E. Wilson, "Biographies," Vought Heritage, 22 January 1931, https://www.vought.org/peopleplaces/html/bcmveew.html.

2. George C. Larson, "The Wasp Engine's Great Leap Forward," *Smithsonian Magazine*, December 2017, https://www.smithsonianmag.com/air-space-magazine/why-the-wasp-is-wonderful-180967115/.

3. Larson, "The Wasp Engine's Great Leap Forward."

4. Bayla Singer, "Engineering Success: Pratt & Whitney Aircraft, 1925–1940," *Business and Economic History* 27, no. 1 (1998), http://www.jstor.org/stable/23703077.

BEISEL'S BENT-WING WONDER

The full-scale mock-up, realistic to minute detail, stood sleek and menacing. . . . I was not overreacting when I gasped at the sight, constantly shook my head in disbelief while fondling every control in the huge cockpit. It was the stuff of dreams, an emotional moment.

—Boone Guyton, test pilot[1]

The XF4U-1 prototype sits on the ramp at Stratford, Connecticut. The small cutout on top of the cowl for the placement of a synchronized .30-caliber gun can be seen just behind the propeller. (NARA)

THE "HOSE NOSE" CORSAIR

Despots were on the march in 1937. The Japanese invasion of China began with the capture of Beijing in July, and Japanese forces quickly pushed deep into the interior of the country. Chinese resistance in the air was crushed by the Japanese A5M fighter, forerunner of the potent A6M "Zeke" from the design team of Jiro Horikoshi at Mitsubishi. Horikoshi's design for the A6M was sketched out that year, benefiting from real-time feedback on the A5M's combat performance.

Around the globe, Germany's Condor Legion was bending the trajectory of the Spanish Civil War with an array of newly operational combat aircraft attached to Spain's Nationalist cause. Among those was an early version of the Messerschmitt Bf 109 that would form the core of the Luftwaffe's World War II fighter force. The Bf 109 compared favorably in speed and firepower to the newest U.S. Navy fighter then in production, the Brewster F2A-1.

These developments suggested to anyone paying attention that air forces of potential future adversaries were not lagging behind but were on pace with new powerful engines, all-metal monocoque-constructed single-wing designs with sleeker profiles, closed canopies, and heavier caliber armament. A common feature of the new European models was liquid-cooled engines, which the U.S. Army Air Corps seemed to prefer as well. The Navy was moving away from liquid-cooled engines by this time. What intelligence could be gleaned from foreign designs induced Navy officials at BuAer to canvass U.S. industry for original, inventive fighter concepts that embodied the latest in aircraft innovation, and kept open the trade space for liquid- and air-cooled engines.

A new fighter solicitation from BuAer appeared in February 1938. This followed a 1936 fighter request that encouraged the move from biplanes to monoplanes. The 1936 announcement yielded a production contract to Brewster for the F2A-1 Buffalo. In that competition, Grumman had clearly misjudged the Navy's intent by submitting a biplane design, but the company was prodded to rework its submission for single-wing configuration. For Grumman, that effort absorbed resources that might otherwise have been thrown into the 1938 response, but it nonetheless yielded what would become the immediate successor to the Buffalo, the Grumman XF4F-2 Wildcat. Another round of new, more powerful engines begat another solicitation in 1937, intended to coax industry to look at improved fighter designs based on twin engines. Grumman found the resources needed to submit a liquid-cooled twin-engine design, the G-25. Lockheed proposed an R-1535 radial-powered variant of its P-38.[2] The Navy passed on both.

From early 20th-century architecture comes the saying "form follows function." Applied to aeronautics, that phrase aptly described the catalyzing effect of engine advances on newer, higher performing aircraft. BuAer's focus was on harnessing the power of a new generation of engines for greater speed. Speed was the new overriding priority, based on the intelligence assessments of the new model fighters in Europe. The bureau, after considerable study, settled on a compromise path that gave the widest discretion to industry in the choice of engine(s) for a new high-performance carrier-based fighter. Companies were asked to submit one or both of two fighter designs: aircraft powered by two modern engines to be selected from an approved list of power plants that came appended to the solicitation, including the turbo-supercharged R-1535 or R-1830 radials, or a single-engine design from the list that also included the Wright R-2600, the Pratt & Whitney XR-2800 radial, and the liquid-cooled Allison V-1710.

The Navy believed that a single Pratt & Whitney R-1830 would not be able to boost speed appreciably beyond what already appeared obtainable in the Grumman XF4F. The Wright R-2600 appeared suitable for some applications, like the Douglas TBD Devastator replacement. But it was hopelessly outclassed in all measures of performance by the XR-2800, the newest Wasp in a line of engines the service was well familiar with. The powerful new Wasp held the most promise but was considered a stretch goal in that it depended on a fairly immature manufacturing process—yet to be qualified—for the cylinder heads.

The Navy remained circumspect about the Allison liquid-cooled engine. Written into the language of the solicitation was as much a concession as BuAer could allow: "An air-cooled engine is preferred, but consideration will be given to a liquid-cooled installation provided a material increase in performance over the air-cooled engine can be shown."[3] This was a tacit recognition of the Army's preference for the liquid-cooled V-1710 engine going into the latest pursuit planes, the P-39 and P-40. The potential scale that could be obtained by greater commonality with the Army's aircraft had great appeal. But the Navy's stand on liquid-cooled engines had been settled years before. They offered some advantage in smaller frontal area for streamlining the airframe, but for shipboard operations, they brought on a host of issues in serviceability, growth, vulnerability, and shipboard storage. The Navy, in 1938, demonstrably leaned toward radials and was especially interested in moving past the R-1800 series to take the power to the next level.

PRATT & WHITNEY R-2800

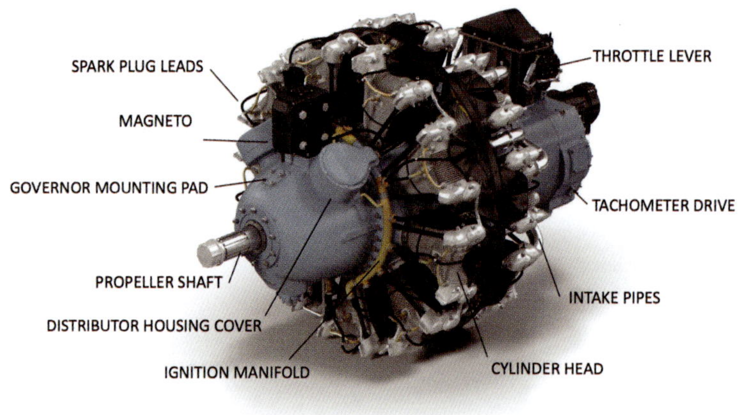

All Corsairs were powered by successive improvements to the basic Pratt & Whitney R-2800 radial engine. Using the same cylinder bore as the earlier R-1340 Wasp, the Double Wasp obtained 2,800 cubic inches displacement by clustering two rows of nine cylinders. With improved cooling heads, it was the first in the family of piston engines to produce one hp per cubic inch of displacement. (Pond5, Inc.)

THE MASSIVE DOUBLE WASP

Pratt & Whitney's success with the first Wasp a decade before relied on a repeatable formula. That formula allowed for increasingly more power without sacrificing reliability, and it set the stage for improved aircraft performance. The XR-2800, a natural evolution that followed the formula, was built with two rows of nine cylinders and displaced 2,804 cubic inches. Power output was greater and weight was less than other competing 18-cylinder models of the time. And the basis for further power upgrades was inherent. Increased performance came without the weight penalty traditionally associated with large radials. The Pratt & Whitney approach relied on cylinder heads built of forged aluminum with integral valve housings shrunk onto forged steel cylinder barrels.[4] The heads were then sheathed in forged aluminum sleeves into which numerous cooling fins were more deeply cut to much finer tolerances. With cooling fin area dramatically increased, forged heads showed lower temperatures for higher compression ratios and higher manifold pressures. That meant lower airflows were required for cooling. In previous radials, cast heads under engine load ran hotter, requiring a greater amount of a richer fuel mixture and more often resulting in engine damage from imprecise detonation.[5]

For the XR-2800 design, the usual solid forged crank was replaced by a "two-piece crankshaft and a solid one-piece master rod; this strengthened the master rod enough to withstand as many revolutions per minute as the pistons could manage, and allowed for a lighter and stronger crankshaft. The crankcase was forged as two halves, the split between them coinciding with the plane of the all-steel cylinders. Accessories, including the supercharger, were all grouped in the back, leaving

Installation of the massive R-2800 Double Wasp in the airplane required the addition of ducting and accessory equipment conformal to the outer mold line that extended the fuselage and contributed to the Corsair's moniker, "Hose Nose." (NARA)

the front of the engine clean. It was this concatenation of design features, none individually new but novel in combination that created an engine of high power and low weight."[6]

VOUGHT'S DESIGN WINS

Performance specifications for the new fighter clearly pointed to Navy expectations that a new class of fighting aircraft was entirely within reach. Speed was specified as highest attainable (speeds well in excess of 300 mph were thought to be possible and highly desired), takeoff distance of 200 feet with wind-over-deck of 25 knots, and stalling speed of not more than 70 mph in a power-on condition for the two-engine design and power-off for the single-engine. Range was specified as 1,000 statute miles, and armament was to consist of either four guns or three guns with provision for more ammunition. The four-gun layout was to accommodate two .30-caliber machine guns along the centerline of the fuselage, synchronized to fire through the propeller arc, and two nonsynchronized .50-caliber machine guns mounted in the wings.

Here, the Navy's reading of international armament developments was evident. European experience pointed to heavier projectile guns. Industry was given the option of offering replacement of one nonsynchronized .50-caliber gun with a Madsen 23-mm cannon, based on its presumed effectiveness against armored vehicles. Specific mention of the Madsen gun was seen by some as encouraging twin-engine designs that could accommodate the heavier weapon in a central gondola underneath the cockpit. The 23-mm cannon would become an afterthought, soon discarded by the Navy. One of the more unusual requirements was for carriage of 40 anti-aircraft bombs for use against enemy bomber formations. Carried in containers of four bombs each mounted in five containers per side in the wing, they could be released at one time in salvo, or in ripple mode, by container, each container at one-twentieth of a second separation.[7] A window on the underside of the fuselage was stipulated so that the pilot could visually gauge his bomb release. The notion of bombing enemy bomber formations may have been a lingering hangover with very senior naval aviators old enough to remember General Billy Mitchell's *Ostfriesland* demonstration. BuAer very soon realized the impracticality of this requirement, and it was rescinded before production. The bombing window did not get removed until well into production.

Companies were permitted to respond to one or both concepts. Two companies responded with twin-engine designs: Grumman with its G-34 concept powered by two R-1535 engines, and Curtiss with two R-1535s powering a derivative of its A-18 attack aircraft then flying with the Army in limited numbers. Ten single-engine concepts, each designed around a different engine choice, were submitted on 11 April 1938. BuAer evaluated and ranked the candidates as follows:

1. Vought's B model with R-2800
2. Brewster's B model, a V-1710–powered F2A Buffalo derivative

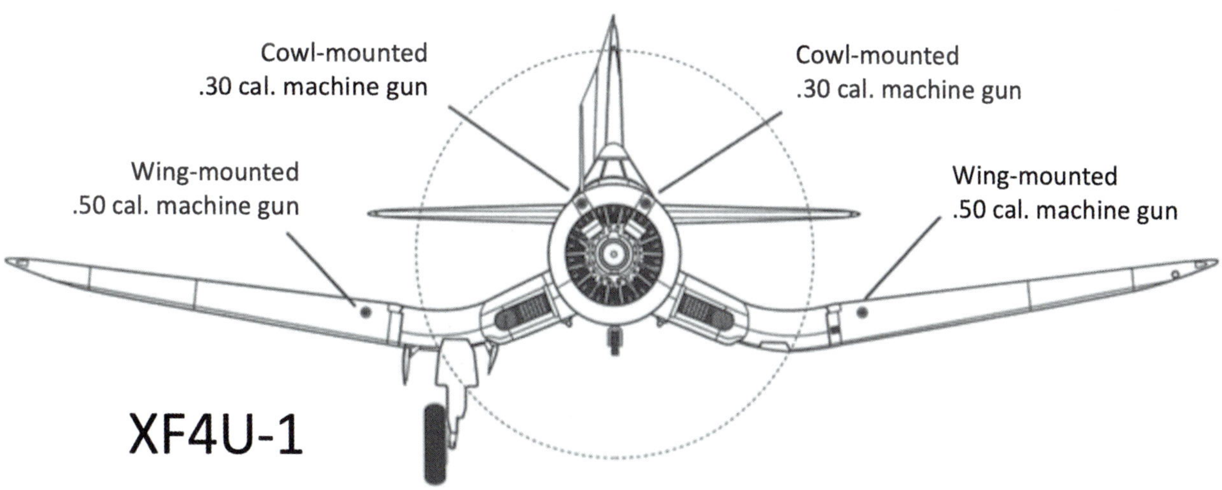

A frontal view of the original XF4U-1 design clearly shows the machine gun arrangement that the Bureau of Aeronautics initially thought to be optimum. (Detail & Scale Copyright Drawing by Lloyd Jones)

An underside view shows the placement of anti-aircraft bomb compartments and the bomb-sighting window that were included in the original solicitation from the Bureau of Aeronautics but soon abandoned. (Detail & Scale Copyright Drawing by Lloyd Jones)

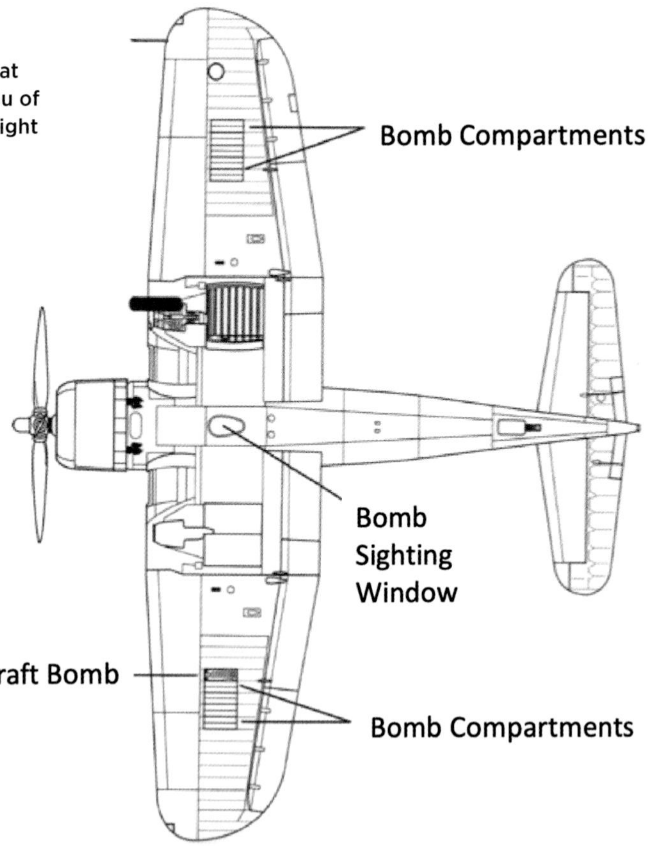

3. Brewster's A mid-wing design powered by the R-2600 engine
4. Vought's A model powered by the R-1830
5. Grumman's single-engine XF4F-2 derivative powered by the R-2600
6. Bell's V-1710 XP-39 derivative
7. through (10) Curtiss designs of various derivatives of the P-36 with different engines.

BuAer, perhaps desiring to cover the spread of possible airframe and engine combinations, elected to award contracts to the first-, fifth-, and sixth-place finishers for construction of flyable prototypes.[8]

Bell's Model 5 would become the single-engine XFL-1 Airabonita, essentially a navalized Army P-39 modified from tricycle gear to tail dragger for arrested landings. Figuring to leverage commonality with and Army support for the XFL-1, Bell retained the Allison XV-1710 V-12 liquid-cooled engine mounted amidships over the wing box. Power was transferred by a 10-foot drive shaft that ran under the cockpit floor to the front-mounted propeller. Armament consisted of a .50-caliber gun fired through the propeller hub, and two .30-caliber guns mounted atop the nose. Bell's contract for one flyable prototype was the last to be awarded in November 1938, which put their flight test program behind the other two awardees. Flight-testing was further held up by late deliveries of V-1710 engines, and then performance problems new constraints. Lower stall speed for carrier landings necessitated a larger redesigned wing. The unconventional internal arrangement that placed the engine behind the pilot meant redesigned tail surfaces to restore stability. As the weight of forward-positioned consumables fuel and ammunition lessened in flight, ballast was needed to restore the center of gravity by adding dead weight. Flight-testing revealed additional design shortcomings that could only be addressed by shipping the prototype back to the Bell factory in late 1941. The Navy by this time had narrowed its preference to the Vought XF4U-1.[9]

Grumman, preoccupied with getting the Wildcat into production, opted to cover its bets by responding with a twin-engine fighter option, its model G-34, that would be awarded a prototyping contract in 30 June 1938. The Grumman prototype was given the company designation XF5F-1 Skyrocket. Grumman made one significant change in its design late in the competition by selecting two Wright R-1820 Cyclone engines to replace the R-1535 engines. That proved costly by adding a significant delay. The Grumman prototype was not delivered to the Navy until February 1941, four months after Vought's XF4U-1 had exceeded 400 mph in its test flight program. The XF5F-1's best characteristic proved to be its climb rate, fully 50 percent greater climb acceleration than the XF4U-1. But in all other measures of fighter performance and projected supportability, it was not in the same class as the XF4U-1. The Navy elected not to put the XF5F-1 into production.[10]

Vought's earliest design effort for this new opportunity was given the internal company designation V-166A,

Bell Aircraft defied convention when proposing its XFL-1 Airabonita for the Navy's 1938 carrier fighter solicitation as the only one of ten competing designs powered by the liquid-cooled V-1710. Perhaps for that reason, it was selected by BuAer for prototyping to round out a field of diverse fighter types. (NARA)

BuAer was open to reevaluating twin-engine designs resulting from its 1938 solicitation as a means to obtain greater speed. Of those proposing twins, the Grumman XF5F-1 was selected for prototyping. It had the best climb rate of the competitors but was a distant second to Vought's XF4U-1 in speed, ceiling, and range. (NARA)

built around the already mature Pratt & Whitney R-1830 engine. The Navy had experience with the R-1830 engine in the Douglas TBD torpedo bomber, but for the 1938 fighter solicitation, BuAer made clear it was looking beyond to what might be attainable with the big R-2800. Vought's chief engineer and design team leader Rex Beisel knew his Navy customer and intuited their preference for the R-2800. He directed his team to give priority to a parallel configuration that relied on the still experimental XR-2800–4 Double Wasp, thus creating the foundation for the V-166B airplane design. Once in possession of the early projected performance data, the BuAer evaluators found the V-166B's potential tantalizing.

The Vought team was thrilled and rightly satisfied to receive a Navy contract on 30 June 1938 for a single flyable prototype based on the V-166B proposal. C. J. McCarthy, Vought's general manager, signed for the company, and Rear Admiral Arthur Cook signed for the Bureau of Aeronautics. Construction of a nonflying mock-up proceeded in parallel with detail design for the flyable prototype. For the flying prototype, designated the XF4U-1, Vought received the sum of $237,505, with an incentive provision that paid or subtracted $60 per pound for every pound under or over the estimated aircraft empty weight up to 100 pounds when delivered. The incentive amount escalated to $100 per pound up to 250 pounds, and if empty weight exceeded or underran the estimate by more than 250 pounds, it was up to the discretion of the Secretary of the Navy to approve contract award. As it happened, the secretary's intervention was not required. But after adjustments for the addition of certain government-furnished equipment, the installation of intercoolers, and the change from XR-2800–2 in Vought's original estimate to a government-provided XR-2800–4 engine upon delivery, the airplane's empty weight was exceeded slightly. Vought grudgingly ponied up a small payback on weight, an acceptable propitiation given the opportunity space that now opened for the company.

Payment under the contract also provided $81,000 for a full set of design drawings, another $40,000 for test data that conformed to BuAer's standard formats, and $5,295 for a one-twelfth-scale model to be delivered to the National Advisory Committee for Aeronautics (NACA) for testing at Langley, Virginia.[11] The committee's 12-foot free-flight tunnel, then nearing completion, was assumed to be the destination for the mostly balsa wood model to test stability and control of the design for predictive correlation, with actual full-scale flight tests to come. A requirement of the contract was delivery of the flyable prototype on the ramp at Anacostia Naval Air Station, fueled and serviced for contractor demonstration flights, no more than 360 days after

BuAer contracted with Vought-Sikorsky in June 1938 for the XF4U-1 prototype, seen here parked near the company's Stratford, Connecticut, plant shortly after completing Navy acceptance trials. (NHHC)

contract award. Navy Board of Inspection and Survey flights would follow to determine if what had been delivered would be satisfactory for service use. Rex Beisel's other evolving design for Vought, the OS2U, looked like a winner for the Navy's ship-based observation aircraft, guaranteeing some production continuity as deliveries of the SB2U dive-bomber wound down. But Kingfisher manufacture was not enough to keep the factory filled at high volume. The XF4U-1 was not exempt from the one truth that held for military aircraft development: Weight will grow, and with it, performance will decline. Everything now depended on Beisel keeping a tight rein on his XF4U-1 design team.

NOTES

1. Boone Guyton, *Whistling Death* (Atglen, PA: Schiffer Publishing, 1994), 23.

2. Tommy H. Thomason, *Bell XFL-1 Airabonita* (Simi Valley, CA: Steve Ginter, 2008), 14.

3. Bureau of Aeronautics, "Class VF Airplanes—Request for Designs and Informal Proposals," amended June 1938. Record Group 72, National Archives and Records Administration, College Park, MD, 40–55.

4. Kimble D. McCutcheon, "Pratt & Whitney Double Wasp (R-2800)," Aircraft Engine Historical Society, 10 March 2002, https://www.enginehistory.org/Piston/P&W/R-2800/r-2800.shtml.

5. Graham White, *R-2800: Pratt & Whitney's Dependable Masterpiece* (Warrendale, PA: SAE, 2001), 185.

6. White, *R-2800*, 185.

7. Bureau of Aeronautics, "Class VF Airplanes," 40–55.

8. Thomason, *Bell XFL-1 Airabonita*, 19.

9. Thomason, *Bell XFL-1 Airabonita*, 29–31.

10. René J. Francillon, *Grumman Aircraft* (Annapolis, MD: Naval Institute Press, 1989), 142–43.

11. Alfred I. Sibila, "Designing the Bent-Wing Bird," *Naval History Magazine* 9, no. 1 (February 1995), https://www.usni.org/magazines/naval-history-magazine/1995/february/designing-bent-wing-bird.

THE FIXED DESIGN VARIABLE: SPEED

When naval air strategists had crafted the requirements for the new fighter, the need for speed had overridden all other performance goals. With this in mind, the Bureau of Aeronautics selected [in the F4U] the most powerful air-cooled engine available, the R-2800.

—Dane Penland[1]

One week after a record-setting flight that exceeded 400 mph, test pilot Lyman Bullard was airborne again in the XF4U-1 prior to official Navy acceptance flights. (NARA)

To extract the maximum energy from the XR-2800's power output, Beisel's engineers at Vought consulted a new Hamilton Standard propeller design manual to size the propeller. The manual pointed to very large propeller blades in conjunction with hydromatic control. Hamilton Standard's Hydromatic innovation marked a major improvement over the counterweight-type, controllable pitch prop, using hydraulic pressure from the engine oil system ported through the nose case to adjust blade angle. For dynamic airplane maneuvering and altitude changes, the Hydromatic regulated blade pitch in flight to maintain constant governed propeller speed.

The team concluded that to minimize propeller blade tip speed compressibility losses while still delivering efficiency throughout all flight profiles up to top speed, a 13-foot, 4-inch propeller would be required. Beisel's aerodynamicists, mindful of reports they were seeing from NACA, determined low wing designs presented more drag penalty than a 90-degree mid-wing join. These seemingly unrelated requirements conspired to drive the configuration to extremely long and heavy landing gear struts with associated retraction mechanisms to provide ground clearance for the arc of the very large propeller.[2]

The issues appeared unresolvable when Beisel called a meeting of his design team leaders in his office. Around Beisel's desk were seated project engineer Frank Albright, lead aerodynamicist and former chief test pilot Paul Baker, lead power plants engineer Jim Shoemaker, and Beisel's understudy Russ Clark. Beisel doodled on a notepad as he weighed the presentations from his engineering disciplines. It was then, on his notepad, that he sketched a possible work-around configuration: Join the wing to the fuselage at a 90-degree angle, thereby minimizing the drag at the corner requiring fillets, but drop the wing-fuselage intersection to a lower position on the fuselage so that the inner wing points down. At the downward end of the inner wing, landing gear could be shortened and prop clearance assured. Then, the outer wing angled up to restore dihedral. This was the moment of conception for the angular inverted gull-wing design that would distinguish the latest Corsair. Beisel's bent-wing doodle was adopted, and his team leaders returned to their design work with renewed resolve.

Experience had conditioned Beisel to appreciate that the new engine could only be coaxed to deliver unprecedented speed when all of the engineering disciplines collaborated closely to minimize drag. To that end, airframe contours had to be squeezed to present the smallest possible frontal area behind the massive engine cylinder heads and cowling. This, in turn, required subsystem designers to repackage accessories and flight mechanical features to fit inside any available space so as not to protrude into the air stream. The shorter landing gear was made to retract rearward by means of a shrink-link that twisted the strut 90 degrees on retraction so that the wheel assembly recessed in a flat position, fully faired in and covered by outer doors. This further reduced drag. This also freed space at the leading edge of the inner wing near the fuselage to place intake ducts for engine oil coolers as well as cooling air for supercharger and carburetors. Air scoops extending into the air stream and raising drag count were thus eliminated. Induction air from the leading edge is channeled through a 90-degree turn entering the wing, where six flow splitters are arranged to smooth out the airflow. Induction air making the turn and traveling over the splitters tended to propagate a high-pitched "scream" when the airplane made high speed. This would be discovered in flight test, but in the fleet the scream would lend to the adoption of the F4U's nom de guerre, "Whistling Death."

FIRST FLIGHT

The prototype was ready for its first flight on 29 May 1940. Parked on the ramp at Bridgeport Airport, it was adorned in body paint reminiscent of the standard color scheme of fleet airplanes a decade before: fuselage in silver and wing tops in chrome yellow. Fuel and oil had been serviced. At the controls for the inaugural flight was Vought test pilot Lyman Bullard. Despite tearing off two elevator trim tabs in flight, Bullard wrestled the wounded beast back for a perfect landing, declaring in the wry, understated manner of seasoned test pilots, "It's some flying machine."[3] Four flights later, junior test pilot Boone Guyton, like Bullard a former Navy carrier pilot, had his turn for a series of low-level, high-speed cabin pressure tests to assure canopy integrity. Deteriorating weather and low fuel state plagued Guyton's first flight, forcing him to bring the airplane down on a golf course fairway. The big XF4U-1 upended as it

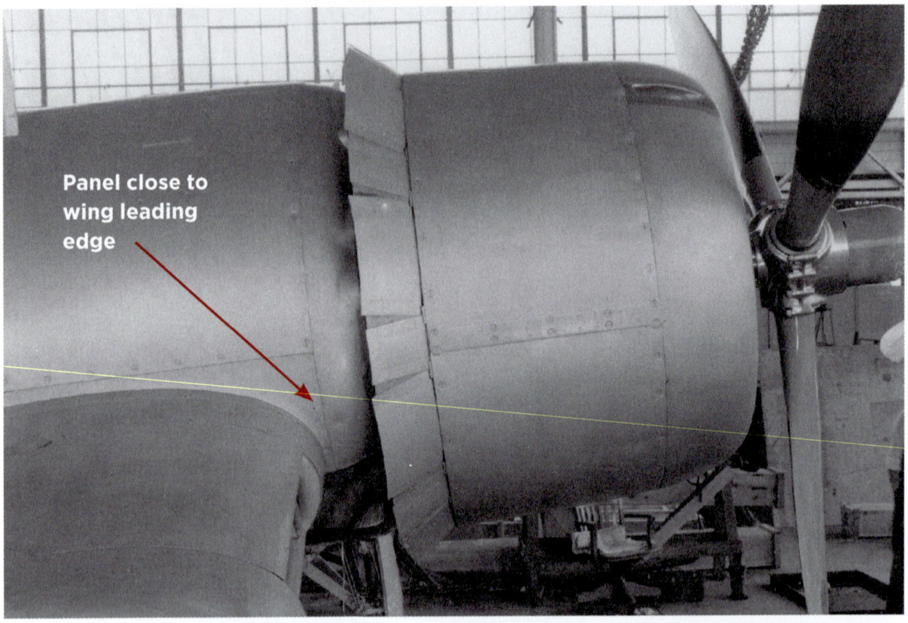

When the prototype XF4U-1 was repaired from Boone Guyton's crash landing, minor modifications appeared that resulted from aerodynamic refinements. These before-and-after comparison photos show that the engine was moved forward 4.5 inches for more distance between wing leading edge and cowl flaps. (Courtesy of Tommy Thomason)

The corners of the wing root inlet for supercharger and oil coolers became more rounded after initial drag cleanup going from the XF4U-1 to the production F4U-1. (NARA)

left the fairway, incurring major damage to plane and pilot. The 360-day post-contract delivery commitment would have been abrogated had the Vought factory team not put in the requisite 24-hour days to repair the crash damage. Three months later, the wounded bird had been restored to test-ready condition, but with a few minor modifications from the original. For example, the engine was moved 4.5 inches forward and the exhaust stack modified, a slightly different propeller configuration was added at the front that broadened the blade tips, and the wing root inlet for supercharger and oil coolers was given a more rounded profile. The reinstalled rudder's aero balance did not extend as far forward, and the elevator grew in chord width.[4] Bullard took the controls once more on 1 October 1940 to set a blistering speed of 405 mph.

Guyton now took over as the XF4U-1 project pilot, and Russell Clark was elevated to chief project engineer behind Beisel to oversee modifications resulting from flight-testing. When changes were required to the original XF configuration, Clark endorsed those for inclusion in the production-

Boone Guyton—Naval Aviator and Vought Test Pilot

Boone Guyton's fifth flight in the new XF4U-1 in July 1940 was nearly his last. Deteriorating weather and low fuel state meant a hasty return and an approach in light rain. He hydroplaned across a golf course into a tree line, upending and overturning to an inverted stop. Vought's only experimental prototype required a complete remanufacture, but Guyton would recover to eventually take over as Vought's principal F4U test pilot.

Guyton graduated from Central Methodist College in Missouri, where his athleticism as a football wide receiver earned him all-conference honors in 1935. Like so many youngsters of his era, he had been enthralled by Charles Lindbergh's solo crossing of the Atlantic in 1927. When he found out about the Navy's new aviation cadet program, he immediately applied and was accepted.

Bombing Squadron Two was Guyton's first assignment, where he flew the nimble Boeing F4B-4 from USS *Lexington*, until transitioning to the Vought SB2U. When his three-year commitment was up, he signed on with Vought as a production test pilot for the SB2U, where his duties took him to France to test-fly reassembled dive bombers for the French and to familiarize French pilots with the airplane. The declaration of war between France and Germany forced an early exit from France, after which he signed on with TWA and flew DC-3s. An offer of employment as a full-time Vought test pilot soon arrived, signed by chief engineer Rex Beisel.

Guyton spent weeks with Navy and Marine pilots familiarizing them with the F4U's idiosyncrasies, and in the process, he formed a lifelong friendship with VF-17 skipper Tom Blackburn. Once back at Vought, Guyton hosted new consultant Charles Lindbergh and spent many hours with the "Lone Eagle" at the airfield at Bridgeport, Connecticut, and at dinner in his home, where they became close friends.

At its wartime peak, Vought employed 23 test pilots in production and experimental work on the Corsair, all under the careful tutelage of Boone Guyton. After the war he would test-fly Vought's first jet, the F6U, with his last test flight taking place in 1951 from the company's new home in Grand Prairie, Texas.

Vought test pilot Boone Guyton stands next to an early production F4U-1, wearing overalls over civilian dress with a standard Navy leather flight helmet of the era. (Vought Aircraft Company Collection, University of Texas at Dallas)

ready aircraft to ensure a quick start once the Navy transmitted authorization. For the rest of the fall and early winter of 1940–41, the test team was charged with conducting contractor test flights to prepare for the Navy's prototype flight evaluations, to include structural tests in dives and accelerations, spin tests, and takeoff and landing measurements. Just days after Bullard's record-setting speed run, Guyton welcomed a Navy flight test team to Vought to begin their familiarization with the prototype before it was handed off formally in February 1941. Involving the Navy test team this early and in the middle of the contractor's test program was contrary to past practice but was viewed as essential by the Navy's chief test pilot, Lieutenant Commander Frederick "Trap" Trapnell. In order to deliver a war-ready airplane in the shortest time, it was necessary to work test issues in parallel with Vought so that Navy preferences could be recognized in the modification process before production plans were fixed.

Early Navy test flights confirmed, and in some cases revealed, issues that were picked up again in the formal service acceptance trials at Anacostia Naval Air Station in the spring of 1941. Acceptance trials found the XF4U-1 "performance characteristics superior in most respects to any fighter previously submitted for test."[5] But the report noted that there were serious flaws that could well result in denial of a production contract if not addressed: poor cockpit visibility due to window arrangement and the long aircraft nose, inadequate roll rate, inadequate firepower, insufficient fuel capacity, and an extreme power-on stall condition that unexpectedly rolled the aircraft on short final for landing—this despite passing marks from the Naval Aircraft Factory in Philadelphia that did most of the carrier arrestment assessments.

The F4U-1 entering the National Advisory Committee for Aeronautics' full-scale tunnel for drag cleanup study. (NARA)

CONDITIONAL NAVY ACCEPTANCE

Lieutenant Commander Trapnell and his Navy flight test team were already working closely with Guyton, Russ Clark, and the Vought team to catalog discrepancies, mindful that practical engineering fixes were critical to award of a production contract. Beginning with fuel capacity, the big XR-2800–4 was indicating a consumption rate for fuel at combat power that was three times that of the Grumman F4F.[6] All agreed that more fuel could be made available if the wing tanks were moved to a 237-gallon fuselage tank in front of the pilot. Other cavities were found to add more tankage to bring the total to 363 gallons. This necessitated moving the pilot's position 32 inches further aft, exacerbating an already difficult visibility problem for the pilot. The near-term fix was to elevate the pilot's seat by 7 inches. There was discussion of changing to a blown bubble-type canopy similar to the British Spitfire, but that was not viewed as a limiting factor for the production decision and would come later. With the fuselage fuel tank now occupying space previously reserved for a .30-caliber and a .50-caliber gun, those guns could now be moved to the wings. With more real estate available in the wings, the .30-caliber guns were up-rated to .50-caliber. Two more .50-caliber guns were added to bring the total to six, three to a side, this in reaction to fresh reports of air combat in Europe and the need for more firepower.

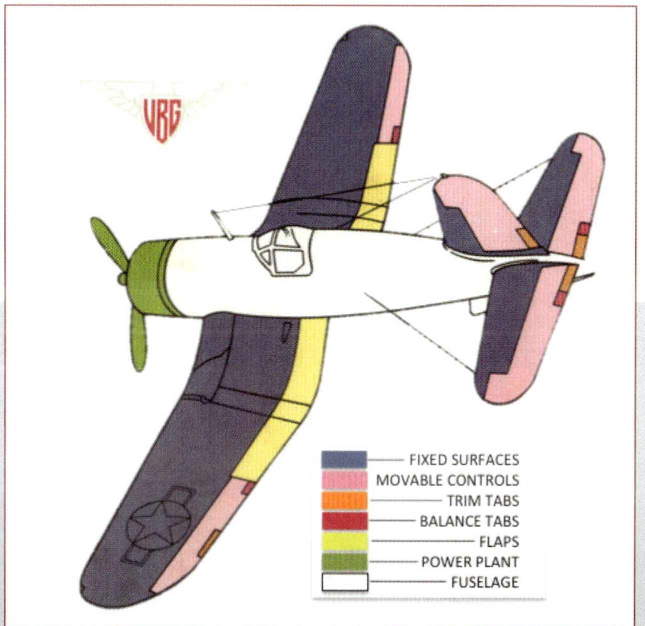

A Vought-Brewster-Goodyear committee general procedure handbook was published to codify and standardize employee understanding of key Corsair component parts. (Aircorps Aviation, Inc.)

The F4U-1 undergoing testing in the early summer of 1943 over the Connecticut countryside. (NARA)

Moving the pilot's cockpit back also alleviated a second sizing issue not directly related to placement of the fuselage fuel tank. The prototype XF4U-1 was powered by the prototype XR-2800–4 engine. This early version of the Double Wasp power plant was delivered with a single-stage, single-speed supercharger. With the arrival of the production version of the engine, space had to be found to accommodate a different arrangement of engine accessories that now included a two-stage supercharger and dual air-to-air

A Vought production test pilot slides into the cockpit of an early production F4U-1. (Rudy Arnold Collection, Smithsonian National Air and Space Museum)

intercooler. The repositioned cockpit simultaneously solved two design issues, but underappreciated by the design team at this point was the critical problem now created by lack of pilot visibility that would vex early operators.

A most fundamental requirement for a fighter airplane was high roll rate, which the XF4U-1 failed to deliver. Lieutenant Commander Trapnell, as the final test authority, insisted that roll rate be improved before acceptance flights could conclude. Vought's aerodynamicists and flight test team redoubled their efforts. Guyton started his flight tests at 6,000 feet and, with rudder blocked, rolled right 2 inches, noted the force on a strain gauge, reset to level flight, then rolled 4 inches, noting the force, straightening out, and repeating. After each flight, he'd debrief the aerodynamicists, who would recalculate and head to the shop, where technicians would trim nose balances on the ailerons. Longer ailerons were fabricated and attached. Every test flight yielded an incremental adjustment to the linkages, trim tabs, and aileron pivot points to lighten the pilot's stick loads as aileron size increased. This process continued for several months throughout the early spring of 1941 wherein most test flights were devoted entirely to roll checks, progressing to full throw of the control stick. Balance tabs were added to fine-tune the aileron movement about its hinge line to produce more consistent lateral forces and, importantly, simplify the manufacturing requirements. Finally, a roll rate greater than 180 degrees per second was obtained, with light stick forces at high speed. The result was satisfactory for contract go-ahead.[7]

Vought received an order for one service test prototype on 30 June 1941, garnering a payment of $69,450 for a test bird to wring out airworthiness of changes to the experimental prototype, including the longer nose that accommodated the fuselage fuel tank, raised pilot's seat with armor, bullet-resistant glass behind the windscreen, new engine accessories, and changes to engine mounts to accommodate the -8 version of the R-2800 that increased engine output from 1,800 hp to 2,000 hp. The two-stage, two-speed supercharger would now push top speed up to 415 mph. The real prize was the provision in the contract for 583 production F4U-1s for $34.7 million, averaging out to just under $60,000 for each aircraft. Production ramped up slowly only due to the nature and sheer number of the design changes required. Included were $6,251 for spares, which, in light of contemporary sparing support models, was woefully short of sustaining early combat deployments.[8] Noteworthy at this point was that nothing was yet documented as a deficiency requiring corrective action for the violent power-on stall tendency. It was dismissed as addressable through pilot training. This failure to attend to a presumed serious safety of flight issue would complicate the Corsair's initial carrier deployment with the Navy and limit the airplane's perceived usefulness as a carrier-based fighter long after its introduction with the Marines.

NOTES

1. Dane Penland, "Vought F4U-1D Corsair," Smithsonian National Air and Space Museum, Steven F. Udvar-Hazy Center, Chantilly, VA, https://airandspace.si.edu/collection-objects/vought-f4u-1d-corsair/nasm_A19610124000.

2. Guyton, *Whistling Death*, 13.

3. W. S. Anderson, "Final Report on Service Acceptance Trials of Model XF4U-1 Airplane No. 1143," Vought Aircraft Company Collection, B44/F05, History of Aviation Archives, Special Collections and Archives Division, Eugene McDermott Library, University of Texas at Dallas, 11.

4. Tommy H. Thomason, "Vought XF4U-1 Corsair," Tailhook Topics, 4 September 2013, http://tailspintopics.blogspot.com/2013/09/vought-xf4u-1-corsair.html.

5. Frederick M. Trapnell Jr. and Dana Trapnell Tibbitts, *Harnessing the Sky* (Annapolis, MD: Naval Institute Press, 2015), 86.

6. Trapnell and Tibbitts, *Harnessing the Sky*, 92.

7. Anderson, "Final Report."

8. James D'Angina, *Vought F4U Corsair* (Oxford: Osprey Publishing, 2014), 12.

ENGINEERING FOR PRODUCTION

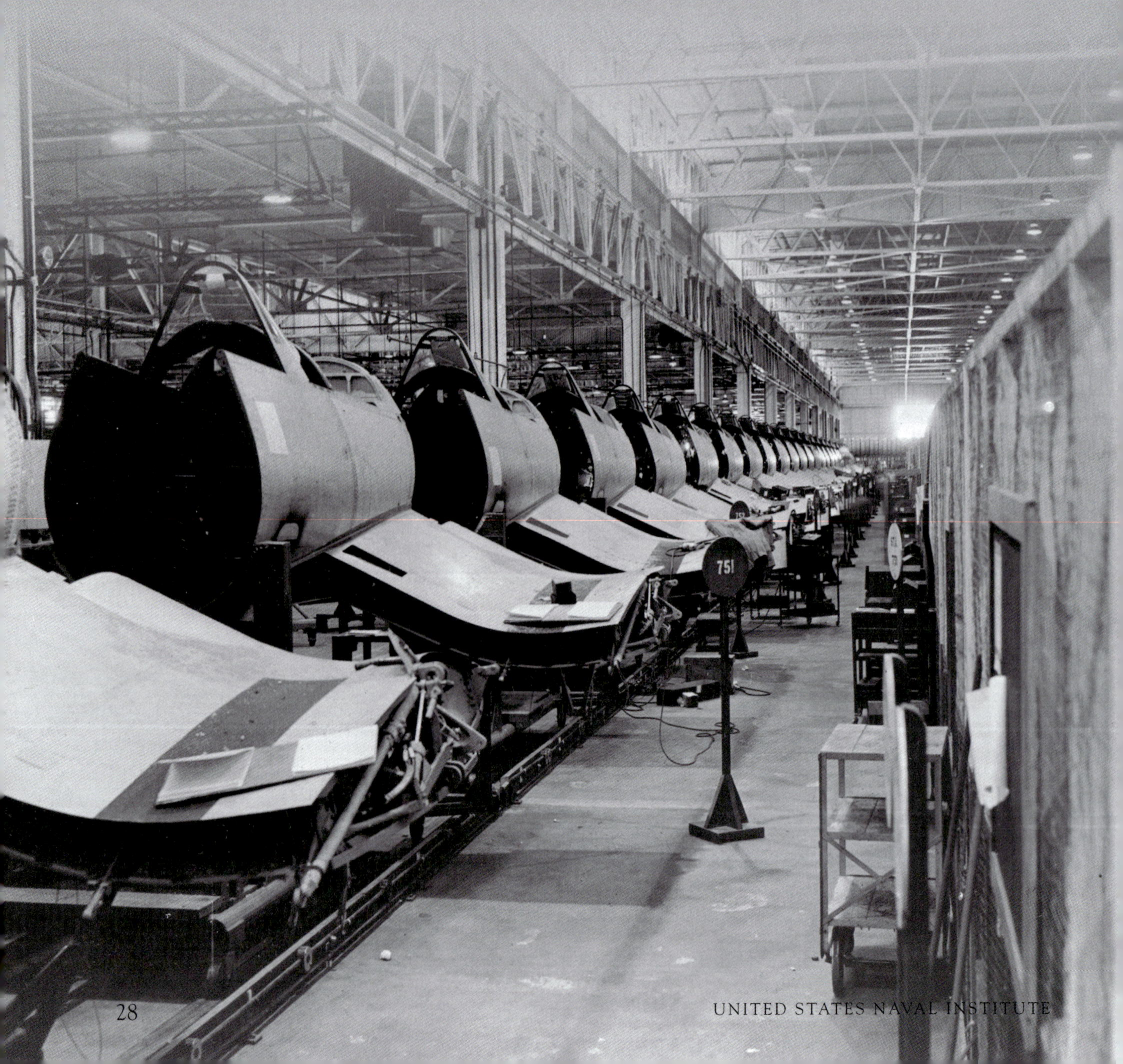

The factory floor was alive with hustling workers and assisting engineers. Coveralled men crawled up and down ladders assembling the big fuselage, cockpit, and engine. On benches nearby, men and women riveted and hammered at a subassembly, secured a Navy inspector's stamp of approval, and started another.

—Boone Guyton, June 1942[1]

PRODUCTION GETS UNDERWAY

A daunting challenge for Vought's manufacturing engineers was designing the curved wing beam for efficient production on the factory floor. The result was an outsize jig fixture that accommodated the main spar, firewall bulkhead, and inner wing accessories. For series production, multiple wing center sections were placed in jig fixtures mounted on a conveyor system that ran the length of the plant. The conveyor was fed by two looped production lines, an inner loop that joined middle and aft fuselage sections and outer loop that joined inner wing and forward fuselage sections, after which it returned to feed the long final assembly line where the cockpit was installed with adjoining electrical and hydraulic lines. The airplane was not built at a single point. Rather, it was constructed in continuous steps as it remained in constant motion, moving nearly imperceptibly at eight inches per minute.

Parts arriving from outside vendors—outer wing panels for Goodyear FG-1s from Briggs in Detroit and wing center sections for Vought F4Us from Willys in Toledo, for example—were positioned to intersect the moving conveyor at the appropriate points. After uncrating on arrival from Pratt & Whitney, engines were mounted on their own assembly line to receive cowlings, starters, generators, pumps, solenoids, and exhaust tubes. Jig assemblies branched off on a siding to receive their engines and then returned to the main conveyor assembly line. The plane was suspended from overhead trolleys for the first half of its travel, whereupon it returned to the floor to continue on its own wheels to completion.[2]

As the conveyor system moved along, workers walked alongside or rode on ladders attached to the jig assembly. As the movement reached the end of a discrete segment, the ladders were detached and moved back to the start of that segment for the next airplane in line. In all, 71 stations allowed different production line specialists a fixed time to swarm over the jig to add their particular equipment. Nearing the end of the line, flight controls were attached and rigged for proper angles. Hydraulic lines were charged so that wing fold tests and landing gear drop tests could be checked on the jig on the factory floor. Rolling off the conveyor line, a finished airplane was towed to the paint shop for its bluing and insignia. Painting completed, it rolled to an outdoor servicing apron where armorers installed and bore-sighted the machine guns. A finished aircraft was towed to the flight line for servicing with engine oil and fuel for engine run-up. The only remaining action for the manufacturer was the functional check flight, at the completion of which the company pilot signed off on the aircraft as ready for delivery.[3]

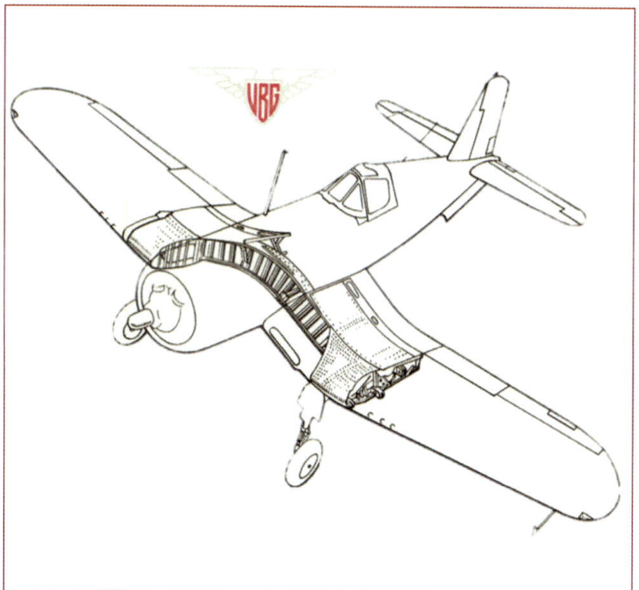

This graphic from the Vought-Brewster-Goodyear general procedure handbook introduced workers at all three final production sites to the importance and positioning of the curved wing center section. (Air Corps, Inc.)

On the outer production line loop at Vought in Stratford, Connecticut, front sections have been mounted on center sections, and the subassembly is moving toward electrical and hydraulic installations. (NARA)

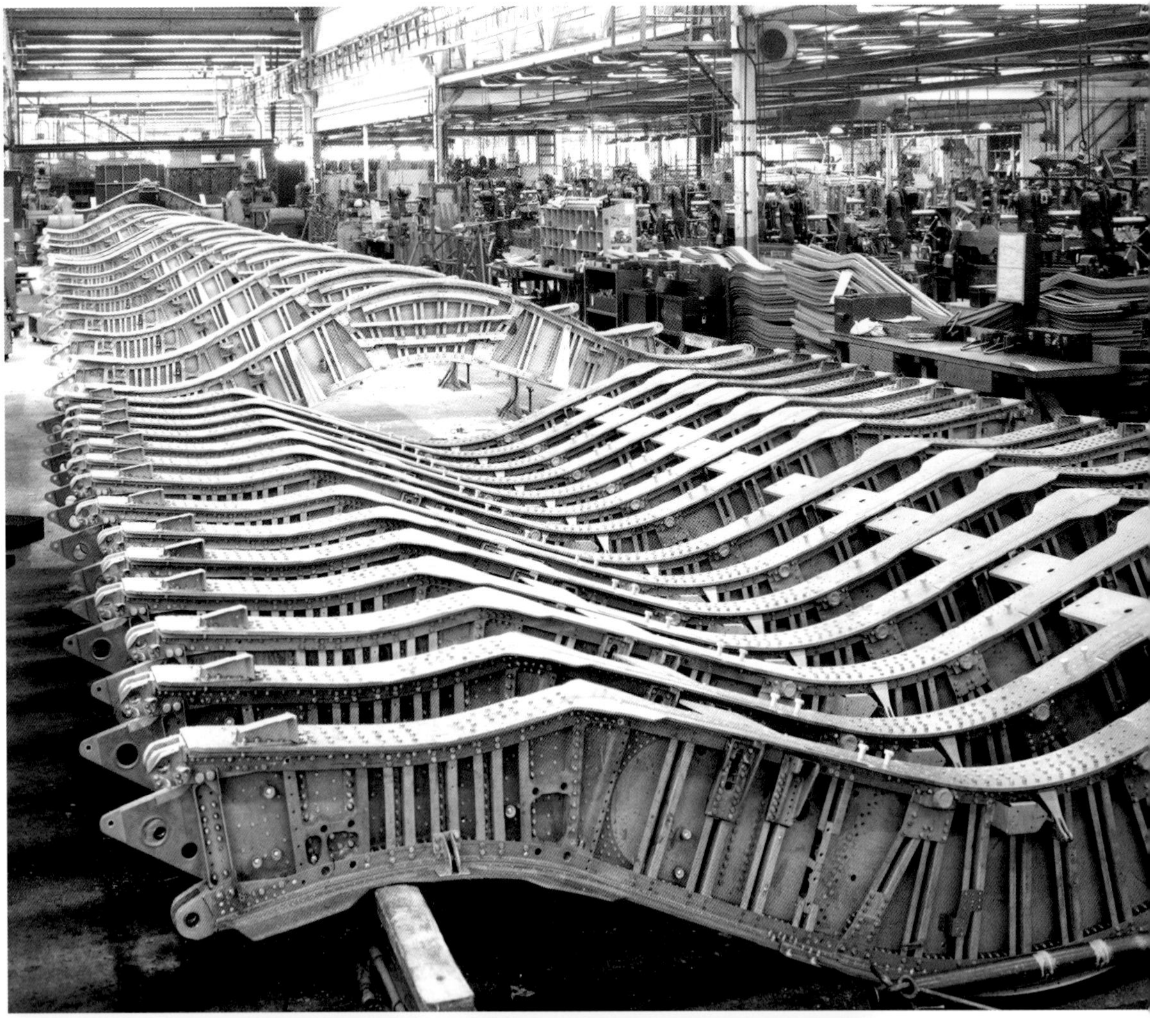

Wing center spars are positioned to join the production line at Vought. (Northrop Grumman Corporation and Smithsonian National Air and Space Museum Archives)

On the Vought outer production loop, center fuselage sections receive electrical and hydraulic connections. (NHHC)

In a production side loop at Vought, power plant technicians affix starter, generator, and exhaust tubing to the R-2800 engine prior to it rejoining the airplane production loop. (NHHC)

At Goodyear, completed engine builds are in flow toward the airplane production assembly line. (Moreno Aguiari, Ambroworks, Inc.)

A perspective on the outer production loop at far right, the inner production loop to the immediate right with center fuselages, and the main production line center-left where engines will be added farther down this line. Note the wheeled scaffold that permitted access to elevated cockpits. (NARA)

A nearly completed airplane approaches the end of the main production line. Factory floor technicians at this point are completing electrical and hydraulic line connections. (NARA)

Final functional checks are made on hydraulic and electrical connections near the end of the line at Goodyear. A technician in the foreground works with a hydraulic accumulator to power up the airplane for landing gear retraction and drop test. (Moreno Aguiari, Ambroworks, Inc.)

Vought F4Us continue down the production line. The technician on the scaffolding is adjusting the new framed bubble canopy. (Vought Aircraft Company Collection, University of Texas at Dallas)

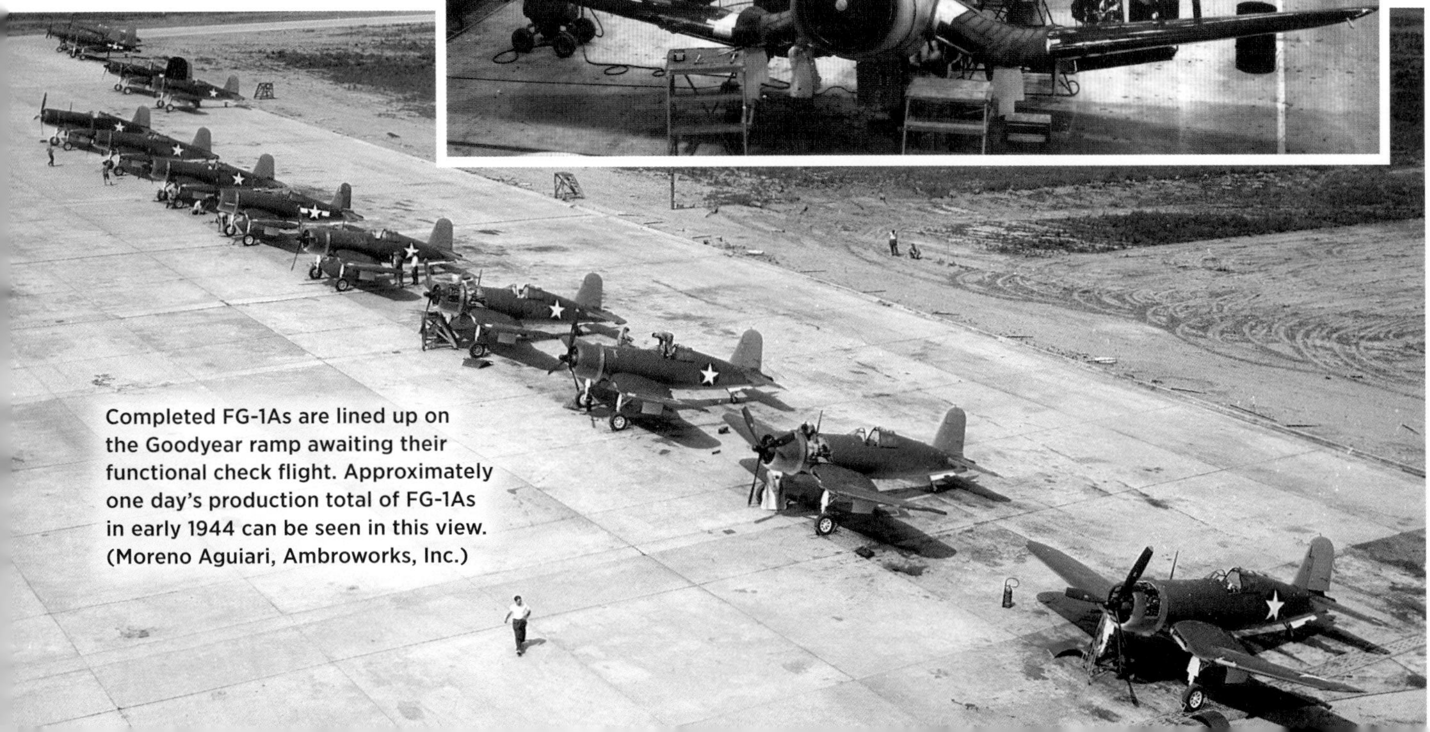

Completed FG-1As are lined up on the Goodyear ramp awaiting their functional check flight. Approximately one day's production total of FG-1As in early 1944 can be seen in this view. (Moreno Aguiari, Ambroworks, Inc.)

PRODUCTION FLIGHT TEST

The single point of interface and accountability to the Navy for acceptance and delivery of a finished Corsair was the production test pilot. Unlike the experimental test pilots, the production test pilots generally flew a prescribed set of checks, referencing a score card on which they confirmed proper functioning of cockpit instruments and switches, takeoff performance for proper indication of rpm and manifold pressure, in-flight engine and flight control performance, and positive action of landing gear and flaps. The test card was derived from an experimental checklist that Boone Guyton had constructed in early developmental flight tests.

When the XF4U-1 was being put through its paces, Lyman Bullard and Boone Guyton were the only test pilots on staff, and they allocated their time in Corsair development work to cover production test flights of other Vought products. When F4U-1s began rolling off the production line, more pilots were needed to meet growing demand for on-time deliveries. Ideally, production test pilots had accumulated a solid engineering background in addition to being excellent pilots. Recruiting of this very specialized category of flight test professionals proved exceedingly difficult against a backdrop of unquenchable demand from the military for pilots in wartime. By May 1942, three more were on staff that included a youngish Charlie Sharpe, who had built up time at a local flying service, and Dick Burroughs and Bill Boothby, both transfers from the engineering staff where they oversaw F4U testing in the low-speed wind tunnel. Two years later, new aircraft were arriving on the ramp at an average rate of nine per day, each requiring a two-hour check flight. Flight test staff had grown to 17 production test pilots and another 6 experimental test pilots for the new series Corsairs.

SECOND SOURCES

With the beginning of World War II in Europe in 1939, President Franklin D. Roosevelt initiated the Protective Mobilization Plan to step up industrial preparedness in the United States. The president called for a productive capacity of 50,000 planes a year.[4] Aircraft engines were a necessary component of that aircraft production expansion. The Navy responded to the president's mandate. By the time XF4U-1 notched its 400 mph flight in October 1940, BuAer's confidence in the R-2800 was such that licensed engine producers were brought on to ramp up for second-source production. In September, the first of those licensed producers, Ford Corporation, was contracted to build out and tool up at its Rouge River site for R-2800 engines. Chevrolet followed, and in short time, Nash-Kelvinator was added to the mix. Ford and Chevrolet engines were earmarked for other aircraft, mostly Army. However, Nash ultimately built 1,790 R-2800–8 engines for early production versions of the F4U built by Vought and other licensed Corsair airframers.[5]

By mid-1941, Vought was in detailed design or early production for Navy aircraft other than the Corsair—the XTBU and OS2U, respectively. Factory floor space at the Stratford site to accommodate the high flow rate of new Corsairs was simply not to be found. To meet wartime demand, licensed production by two second-source contractors, Brewster and Goodyear, was in negotiation. The contracts that resulted from successful negotiations were then the basis for the formation of a Vought-Brewster-Goodyear, or VBG, committee. The committee was an advisory board charged with standardizing all aspects of production between the three Corsair builders. Sponsored by BuAer, the committee was further broken down into subcommittees for engineering, procurement, and production, with Navy representation and oversight over each. Airplane production was segmented into several sections, built separately, with interchangeable parts but to common standards that could be easily transferred between manufacturers or replaced in the field as complete subassemblies. Three units comprised the fuselage: a front section containing the cockpit and fuel tank to which the wing center section was attached, a midsection housing the radio and other avionics components, and a tail section that held the tail wheel and extended rearward for attaching the empennage and tail control surfaces. The wing subassembly was made up of the large curved center section, essentially a beam lying in transverse relation to the fuselage orientation, and the two outer-wing panels that came with wing fold attachments. The wing center section was at the nexus of the airplane buildup, housing the wheels, struts, and retraction mechanism with hydraulic lines, and later, two load-bearing pylons for fuel tanks or heavy ordnance.[6] Brewster was assigned the role of developing a set of manuals that detailed inspection procedures for not just aircraft construction, but also more basic tasks like interpreting blueprints and change orders. Ironically, these basic inspection procedures—or rather, failure of their observance—would be Brewster's undoing.

BREWSTER TROUBLES

Brewster Aeronautical Co. began licensed Corsair production in November 1941, with their Corsair to be identical to the Vought-produced F4U-1 but designated F3A. Brewster's contract for F3A production capped a run of unbridled growth in the late 1930s when it jumped into a rapidly accelerating defense marketplace for aircraft subassemblies. By the late 1930s, the company had secured prime contracts for two Navy aircraft of their own design, the F2A Buffalo and the SB2A Buccaneer. A second factory in Newark, New Jersey, was added to Brewster's original factory on Long Island, primarily for F2A manufacture. The two locations could barely accommodate full rate production for both, and with more prewar work expected, the company scouted for new, dedicated sites away from congested urban areas. For an investment of $9 million, Brewster acquired 370 acres of farmland and constructed a manufacturing facility at Johnsville, Pennsylvania, that would handle F3A production, and the transfer of much of the SB2A and F2A work out of their prior cramped spaces on Long Island and in Newark.

A production contract for $138.6 million committed the company to producing 1,500 F3As. It was not long before the results of too little due diligence on the part of Vought and the Navy would be apparent. A new facility required a sizable work force of experienced aircraft workers, which simply was no longer available with other defense plants already ramping up for wartime levels of output. A rapidly expanding Naval Aircraft Factory and naval shipyard in nearby Philadelphia had already drawn down the potential pool of tradesmen that Brewster could expect to enlist within commuting distance. As a result, much of the workforce that was hired had little to no practical aircraft production experience to handle the new work in addition to the contract obligations on the other Navy aircraft. This became evident when Brewster failed to deliver a single Buccaneer in 1942. Unauthorized labor strikes were faulted. F3A work was similarly slipping. Congressional hearings revealed incidents of sabotage on the floor and profit-skimming by convicted felons who had surprisingly bluffed their way into the executive suite as corporate officers.

Completed F4U-1s await functional check flights after rolling off the Vought production line at Stratford, Connecticut. (Vought Aircraft Company Collection, University of Texas at Dallas)

Five months after the contract award for Corsair production, President Roosevelt authorized the Navy to seize the plant. Retired Navy Captain Conrad Westervelt, former head of Naval Aircraft Factory Philadelphia, was brought back on active duty to temporarily take charge. BuAer chief Rear Admiral John Towers and Assistant Navy Secretary for Air Artemus Gates summoned Reuben Fleet, former head of Consolidated Aircraft, from San Diego to take charge and bring the plant in line. Fleet arrived accompanied by Consolidated colleague C. A. Van Dusen, who, when the Navy relinquished control, was named president. That lasted only about ten months before the company board, under considerable Navy influence, elected industrialist and shipbuilder Henry Kaiser as the new company head in early 1943. Kaiser tried to implement a more union-friendly climate but made little headway. Even after this, Brewster-manufactured F3As were consistently late, and quality declined appreciably. Kaiser's management team was "so worried about poor construction that they built a device to turn over the planes to shake off loose parts and forgotten tools, and planes intentionally shipped with faulty rudders and engines."[7]

Eventually, Brewster produced 735 F3As at Johnsville, but none served in frontline U.S. squadrons. After an initial tranche of Vought-produced F4U-1s were delivered to Britain's Fleet Air Arm as Corsair Is, another 430 Brewster-manufactured F3As would be sent to the Fleet Air Arm as Corsair IIIs. The most distinguishing characteristic, other than the allegedly poor manufacturing tolerances and quality control on the Corsair IIIs, was the clipped outer wing that permitted clearance through hangar deck overheads on British carriers when the Corsair's wings were folded.[8] The U.S. Navy had had enough and terminated Brewster's Corsair contract on 19 May, noting at the time that the man-hour expenditure for the Corsair at Brewster was excessive—9,800 hours to produce a single aircraft, compared to 6,700 at Goodyear and an even lower 4,700 at Vought. This disparity contributed to a sizable dollar difference that came back to the Navy in cost per plane: $72,000 for a Corsair from Brewster, while the Goodyear plane cost $57,000 and Vought's Corsairs were costing $63,000 per plane. Underlying the Navy's dissatisfaction with production man-hours and cost was the added burden of carrying the full financial backing for Brewster for the prior three years, amounting to a $55 million loan for which Brewster had failed to make any loan payments.[9]

Goodyear Aircraft Corporation, by contrast, proved an exemplar of orderly and competent manufacturing. A major difference from Brewster was simply economic scale and longevity, the result of a history of manufacturing primarily rubber and forged aluminum products for the U.S. military

Boone Guyton readies for test flight in an early production F4U-1. (Courtesy of Jeffrey Ethell Collection)

aircraft going back to the Navy's first airships in World War I. By 1940 the rubber business had expanded to include a growing volume of war materiel such as aircraft tires and self-sealing fuel tanks, augmented by contracts for aircraft subassemblies for the Martin B-26 Marauder and Grumman TBF Avenger.

Goodyear Aircraft was a creation of the Goodyear Tire and Rubber Company in 1939, situated adjacent to the Akron, Ohio, rubber works to accommodate more complex aircraft parts. With abundant room for growth, factory floor space quickly grew. However, Goodyear, like Brewster, had difficulty staffing up for full rate Corsair production. Where Goodyear may have had a geographic advantage over Brewster was its location within commuting distance of Cleveland, where there still resided a deep reservoir of workers experienced in machine tool manufacture, petroleum refining, and automobile assembly. Company payroll swelled tenfold with the F4U-1 order to 32,000 factory workers; however, most of that growth came with a need for on-the-job training. For Corsair production, at peak, Goodyear's workforce was 60 percent women, a demographic not unlike other large defense manufacturers.[10] Goodyear's Corsairs were given the designation FG-1 and, with orders for FG-1 and follow-on FG-1D, would eventually surpass 4,000 aircraft.

CARRIER SUITABILITY

The XF4U-1's first encounter with carrier arresting gear did not go well. Test pilot Guyton flew the XF to Naval Air Factory Philadelphia in January 1942 for simulated carrier approaches to arrested landings on the airfield. Russ Clark and Guyton observed as a Navy pilot made the first pass. When the arresting hook grabbed the cross-deck pendant, it completely separated from the aircraft along with the tail wheel. Makeshift repairs permitted testing to go on for three more months, but more trouble in approach and landing was yet to surface. After servicing and repair at Vought, the XF was dropped off with the Navy at Anacostia for completion of acceptance tests. In three months, the first production F4U-1, Bureau Number 02155, took flight on 25 June 1942 from Bridgeport Airport in Connecticut.

The Battle of Midway had been won earlier that month but at some cost. If one lesson of the battle was brought stunningly into bold relief, it was that the Japanese A6M Zeke had ravaged the Navy's F4F Wildcat. Only innovative tactics like the Thach Weave had forestalled an American rout in the air. "Our F4F-4 is markedly inferior to the Japanese Zeke fighter in speed, maneuverability, and climb," wrote Admiral Chester Nimitz to Admiral Ernest King in his post-action assessment.[11] The urgency was palpable for getting the Corsair and Hellcat out to carrier squadrons as quickly as possible. But more carrier suitability trials were in the offing for the Corsair. From initial

Vought test pilot staff, 28 May 1942 (left to right): Boone Guyton, Charlie Sharpe, Dick Burroughs, Bill Boothby, and chief test pilot Lyman Bullard. Boothby perished in a test flight of a Corsair in March 1944. Burroughs did not survive a similar Corsair crash in 1946. (Courtesy of Mary Evans Picture Library, Ltd.)

F4U-1 deliveries, Lieutenant Commander Sam Porter took the seventh F4U-1 aboard USS *Sangamon* (ACV-26) operating in the Chesapeake Bay in September. According to Vought archives, "After four terrifying landings, he called it quits, certain the airplane was on the verge of killing him. The Corsair's cockpit was so far back in its fuselage that Porter found it difficult to see the *Sangamon*'s landing signal officer on the port side of its deck. The fighter's ultra-long 'hose nose' made it nearly impossible for the pilot to get timely feedback to make corrections to his approach. When the Corsair thumped down on the deck, the landing gear's oleos—shock-absorbing struts—bottomed out, then bounced back like giant pogo sticks, causing the airplane to bound over the arresting wires."[12]

This inauspicious start foretold deepening concern in BuAer about the Corsair's ability to land on the ship. As 1942 drew to a close, the Navy had already accepted 178 F4U-1s fresh off the production line, but data reduction from November tests in the NACA full-scale wind tunnel (FST) at Langley, Virginia, was pointing to specific fixes for some of the handling issues. Overall, the goal of the wind tunnel tests was drag cleanup. It was immediately clear that simply faring over some gaps and seams would yield a predicted 12 mph higher top speed. While top speed was important, the more critical information derived from the FST related to carrier approach.

IN-LINE CHANGES

Tests confirmed that different canopy shapes that could help visibility immensely added only incremental but acceptable rise in drag. The current six-paned plastic canopy—not unusual for canopy designs of the late 1930s, but somewhat scornfully derided as the

At Vought, the new bubble strapped canopy is mocked up for fit checks before heading to National Advisory Committee for Aeronautics' full-scale wind tunnel for drag checks. (NARA)

"birdcage"—encased the cockpit in multiple frames, resting on a set of trolley rollers that rode up, then aft, along an extruded track embedded in a "turtledeck" behind the pilot. When closed, it was flush with the aft structure, providing rearward view through the turtledeck only when the pilot craned his neck to peer out. Otherwise, it blocked his vision in turns on the carrier approach. A new canopy design was needed that captured the most recent manufacturing advances. A 5-inch-higher compound-curve, three-panel section was created to ride on the same track fixtures. Transparencies of Lucite or Plexiglas were formed in a new process that used felt-covered wooden molds. The extruded track was replaced with stainless steel to ensure easy opening and closing. The rear windows came out, replaced by more armor for the pilot. The new framed, blown canopy entered production with the 125th airplane on the line, and was retrofitted to the sixth and subsequent airplanes already delivered.[13]

Changing to ailerons with beveled trailing edges showed that roll rate could be increased by 59 percent over the original wooden ailerons. Flow visualization tests revealed that the abrupt stall of the left wing in the power-on condition was due to an increased upwash at the wing leading edge from the wake of the huge propeller. Repeated trials in the tunnel pointed to the application of a small leading edge spoiler to the right wing just inboard of the wing fold line. More flow visualization time in the tunnel indicated a uniform stall pattern for both wings with the spoiler attached, thus easing the nasty surprise of severe left wing drop on short final.[14] Beginning in early 1943, fixes identified in the wind tunnel, and those developed by Vought engineering at the factory, were cut into the production line, resulting in a new series designation for the Corsair: the F4U-1A.

F4U-1As coming down the production lines at Vought, Brewster, and Goodyear beginning in the spring of 1943 benefited from an engine modification from Pratt & Whitney, a water injection system that cooled the cylinders for a momentary boost in power. If the R-2800–8 had an Achilles heel, it was the number 13 cylinder. Connected to the master rod, it would burn hotter after a few minutes of military power setting. If that cylinder in particular could be tamed at the highest power settings, more energy could be coaxed from the engine.

The throttle quadrant mounted just above the pilot's left-hand console featured a lever for mixture settings: *auto lean* for best cruise, *auto rich* for best power, and *full rich* for military power. Full rich ports more fuel into the internal combustion process to help cool the engine for higher manifold pressure. By altering the water content of the fuel/air mixture, the engine gets additional cooling on demand in full rich for even higher manifold pressure. In operation, the pilot advanced the throttle to military power setting and adjusted a switch on the throttle quadrant that activated a regulator to lean out the fuel and inject the proper amount of water for that momentary burst of power. It had its limits. This war emergency power setting could not be used for much longer than five minutes before engine heat began to take over again. The engine bore a new designation: R-2800–8W (*W* for water injection), and the W would appear in later series versions of the R-2800 engine.[15]

NOTES

1. Guyton, *Whistling Death*, 95.

2. "The Navy's Fastest Fighter," Vought Aircraft Company Collection, History of Aviation Collection, University of Texas at Dallas.

3. Thomas Morgan, "The Industrial Mobilization of World War II," *Army History Magazine*, no. 30 (Spring 1994): 31.

4. Graham White, *R-2800: Pratt & Whitney's Dependable Masterpiece* (Warrendale, PA: SAE, 2001).

5. Pennsylvania Bureau for Historic Preservation, "Johnsville Naval Air Development Center History," https://explorepahistory.com/hmarker.php?markerId=1-A-2F4.

6. "The Navy's Fastest Fighter."

7. D'Angina, *Vought F4U Corsair*, 23.

8. D'Angina, *Vought F4U Corsair*, 23.

9. Charles E. Egan, "Expert to Survey Brewster's Plant," *New York Times*, 1 June 1944, 10.

10. "The Navy's Fastest Fighter."

11. John Lundstrom, *The First Team* (Annapolis, MD: Naval Institute Press, 1984), 442.

12. "The Navy's Fastest Fighter."

13. Lew Knapp, "Corsair," *Sikorsky Archives News*, March 2001, https://sikorskyarchives.com/wp-content/uploads/archives-newsletters/NEWS-2001-03.pdf.

14. Joseph R. Chambers, *Cave of the Winds—The Remarkable History of the Langley Full-Scale Wind Tunnel* (Washington, DC: NASA, 2014), https://www.nasa.gov/sites/default/files/files/Cave_of_the_Winds_pdf.pdf, 145–47.

15. Guyton, *Whistling Death*, 136.

SOUTH PACIFIC DEBUT

With the Corsair I had confidence in meeting the Zero and for the most part sensed and felt an advantage.

—Lieutenant Colonel Kenneth A. Walsh, USMC (Ret.)[1]

Joe Clifton's F4U-1s in formation over Southern California. Within weeks of this photo, the squadron would be directed to exchange their Corsairs for F6F-3 Hellcats. (NARA)

CORSAIRS PREPARE FOR WAR

The first three Corsair squadrons had formed by January 1943. Equipped with F4U-1s, they were readying for Pacific deployment: Marine fighter squadron VMF-124 at Camp Kearney near San Diego under Major Bill Gise, Navy fighter squadron VF-12 at North Island under Lieutenant Commander Joe Clifton, and Navy fighter squadron VF-17 at Norfolk commanded by Lieutenant Commander Tom Blackburn. Even as these squadrons accepted their new airplanes, Russ Clark's Vought field team rushed through last-minute fix kits for problems that surfaced in Navy flight tests but did not make it in time to production line changes for the F4U-1A: The seat was raised, a rear-view mirror was added to the canopy, and the engine cowl flap hydraulics were replaced by mechanical controls to minimize fluid blow-back across the windscreen. Boone Guyton visited with the San Diego squadrons to explain the modifications and to tutor the more inexperienced pilots on the Corsair's peculiar handling traits.

Joe Clifton's VF-12 "Peg Legs" qualified in carrier landings aboard USS *Core* (ACV-13) off San Diego and were on their way across the Pacific when, at their en route stop in Hawai'i, they were ordered to exchange their Corsairs for F6F Hellcats for their carrier deployment. The squadron accepted the trade without rancor or pushback, but in its short time with VF-12, the Corsair came to be highly regarded. Squadron executive officer Lieutenant Commander Bob Dosé remembered the Corsair as "a beautiful bird. We estimated it had about 50 knots on the F6F. . . . By comparison, the Hellcat was a baby buggy, but we loved the 'hog,'"[2] The decision to remove the Corsair was made at the highest levels of Pacific command out

Fighter Squadron 12 was the Navy's first to be assigned the F4U-1 in early 1943. Squadron commanding officer Lieutenant Commander Joe Clifton (second from left) briefs the finer points of Corsair rendezvous to attentive squadron pilots. (NARA)

of a concern that adequate provisioning of spares and support training had not yet been put in place. Even though F6F deliveries to the first operational Hellcat squadrons were occurring roughly in parallel, the urgency to rush a new fighter into the Pacific theater was such that the Hellcat's more docile handling skewed the spares and support funding to the F6F. So even as the Corsair's handling quirks were being addressed, the sparing, support, and training were not.

CARRIER SUITABILITY CONCERNS PERSIST

Doubts about the Corsair's handling in the carrier environment continued to dog the plane's introduction, even as its quirks were being addressed with identified engineering changes. More testing was ordered in March aboard the side-wheel training carrier USS *Wolverine* (IX-64) operating on Lake Michigan. Results reported by the Naval Air Station Glenview carrier training unit to BuAer were promising: "F4U airplane is an excellent carrier type and very easy to land aboard. It is no different than any other airplane. Performance in arresting gear very similar to that of TBF airplanes landing at same time with same settings and pressure."[3]

As qualification tests were getting underway on *Wolverine*, VF-17 skipper Blackburn took his squadron aboard USS *Charger* (ACV-30), steaming in the Chesapeake Bay. Little to no feedback from VF-12 or the Glenview unit had been shared with Blackburn, but he had put the squadron through a dozen sessions of simulated carrier landings with their Corsairs at an auxiliary airfield near Norfolk. Blackburn's first landing on *Charger* exposed the wing drop and the bounce, sending his airplane 20 feet in the air before coming back down, smacking the deck, and grabbing the number one wire. Four more landings were needed for qualification, and they went satisfactorily once Blackburn got past the jitters of his first carrier landing in the Corsair. The squadron experienced broken tail wheels and blown tires, but all qualified by making their five arrested landings.[4]

VF-17 remained ashore waiting for the arrival of USS *Bunker Hill* (CV-17) on her shakedown cruise. The squadron left the Norfolk area and moved to an auxiliary air station at Manteo, North Carolina, to continue training. At Manteo, VF-17 maintenance officer Lieutenant (junior grade) Butch Davenport was joined by Russ Clark and his Vought field rep to remedy some of the persistent gripes. For the hard bounce, Clark messaged daily with the full team of Vought engineers in Stratford, hammering out a mitigation strategy. By incorporating a release valve that balanced air pressure

VF-17 carrier qualifications resumed on board USS *Bunker Hill* (CV-17) off the U.S. East Coast in July 1943. The Corsair is again exhibiting the tendency for the left wing to prematurely and unexpectedly stall immediately before touchdown on the flight deck. (NARA)

and hydraulics, a softer oleo piston stroke with greater air pressure could be realized. Finally, to address one aspect of the visibility complaints, the top three cowl flaps behind the engine were battened down to eliminate the spray of hydraulics and engine oil that clouded the windscreen. A big change for improved visibility was coming but not until the 689th-production F4U-1, raising the cockpit seven inches and installing a bulged canopy, along the lines of the Malcolm hood used on Spitfires. This was a big help with visibility from the cockpit, replacing the original birdcage framed canopy to provide a better all-around field of view. Finally, a lengthened tail wheel strut flattened the airplane's three-point stance, improving the pilot's line of vision over the nose. The raised tail wheel simultaneously corrected for a sudden yaw on touchdown that was a result of the wing stall and ground effect.

Some adjustments would make it immediately into already delivered F4U-1s as field modifications, but most would be standard in production versions of the F4U-1A model. On *Bunker Hill*'s return to port in Norfolk, VF-17's new F4U-1As were waiting to be picked up at Floyd Bennett Field in New York for the flight back to Norfolk. With landing quals completed on *Bunker Hill*, Blackburn and *Bunker Hill* commanding officer Captain John Ballentine were disheartened to see a message from Commander, Air Forces Atlantic Fleet Vice Admiral Pat Bellinger offering VF-17 the option of replacing their Corsairs with F6F Hellcats en route to the theater of operations. Before releasing a formal reply, Ballentine asked for Blackburn's honest assessment. The VF-17 skipper responded; "I recommend in the strongest terms that we go forward with the Corsairs. The F4U is the better combat airplane."[5] Blackburn may not have realized at that moment that he was committing the squadron to shore basing. Days before their departure, Commander, Naval Air Forces Pacific Vice Admiral John Towers transmitted his intention to BuAer's chief Rear Admiral Dewitt Ramsey: "In order to simplify spares problem . . . assign all Corsairs to Marines and equip Fightrons or medium and light carriers with Hellcats."[6] The bottom line was that VF-17 kept their Corsairs, but the squadron was ordered off *Bunker Hill* once it arrived in Hawai'i to await ferry by escort carrier to the South Pacific.

WHISTLING DEATH ARRIVES

Unencumbered by a need for carrier qualifications, Bill Gise's VMF-124 had departed for the South Pacific in January 1943. Carrier qualifications aside, the squadron of mostly newly winged aviators barely had time to adjust to their new mounts. The squadron was declared com-

Fighter Squadron 17 was the other Navy unit to be assigned the Corsair. VF-17 qualified for carrier landings on board USS *Charger* (ACV-30) on 8 March 1943. Here, VF-17's number 6 experienced the F4U's tendency to bounce on touchdown. (NARA)

Marine Fighter Squadron 124 was the first F4U unit to make a combat deployment. Squadron aircraft are lined up on Marston matting at the Fighter One airstrip on Guadalcanal in early April 1943. (NARA)

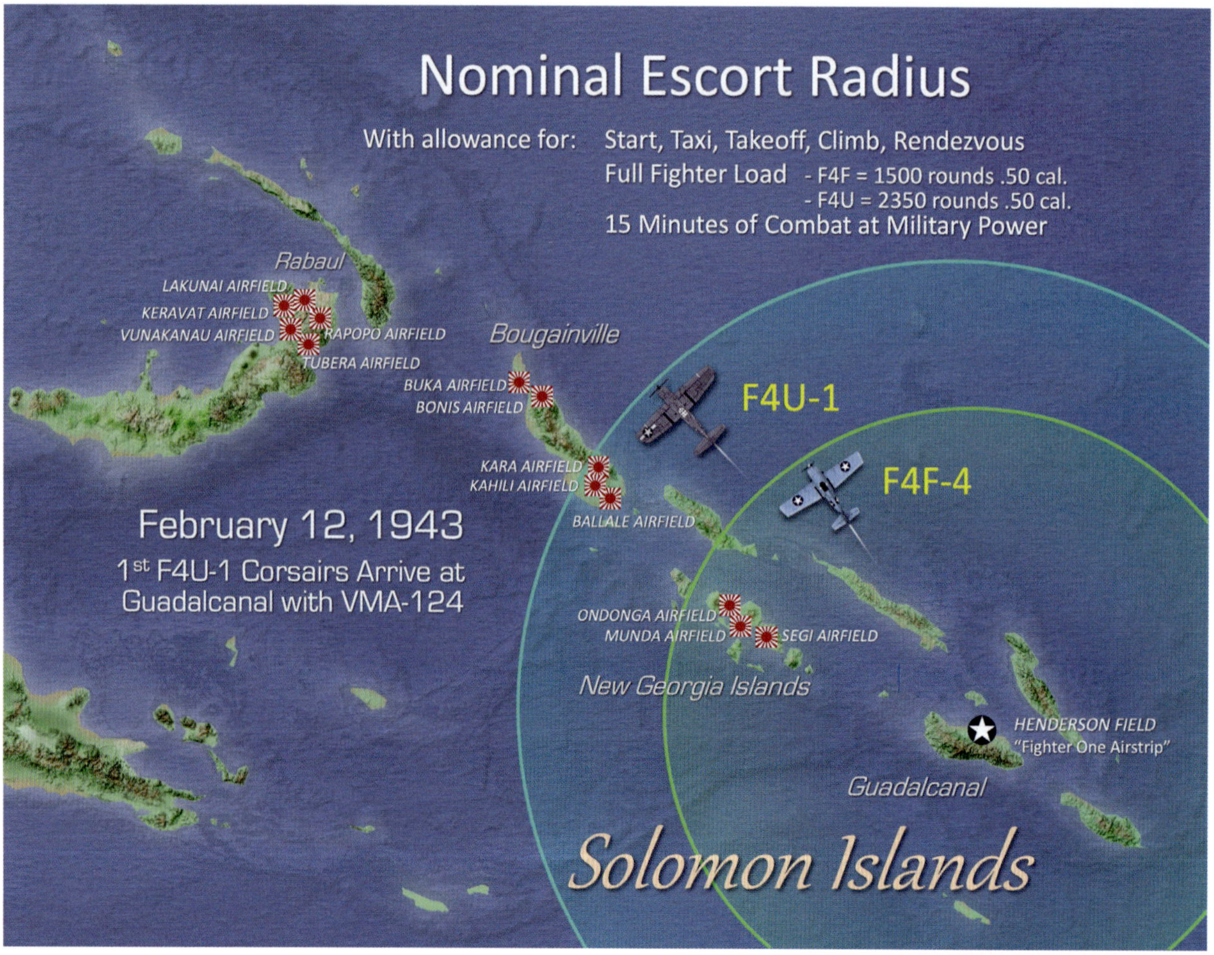

The arrival of the Corsair with VMF-124 changed the calculus. Strike aircraft could now expect fighter escorts to accompany them to targets at greater range up the Solomons chain of island bases than was possible with the F4F-3 or -4. (Graphic artwork by Aldo Spadoni)

bat-ready prior to leaving San Diego when the average squadron time in the Corsair was 20 hours. Many had not yet fired the guns in the F4U when the squadron boarded its transport for the South Pacific. Squadron planes were ferried from San Diego via Hawai'i on the deck of aircraft transport vessel USS *Kitty Hawk* (AKV-1) to a staging base on Espiritu Santo, Vanuatu. Pilots arrived by ship and aircraft transport, to ready the airplanes for the flight from Espiritu Santo to Guadalcanal. Two weeks were spent removing preservation slime from the airplanes and attending to nagging gripes on the F4Us, mainly radio interference from the ignition system and inadequate pressurization of the ignition at altitude. Sparking would jump the distributor gap and burn out the points, causing engine failure. Lieutenant Ken Walsh flew the maintenance check on the ignition problem, lost the engine, and rode the airplane into the sea to be picked up by a PBY. By adding an air pump to each distributor housing, further ignition problems were minimized. Short-term fixes sufficed to sustain the squadron's preparation, permitting 17 squadron F4U-1s to fly on to Guadalcanal's Fighter Two airstrip on 12 February 1943. Two hours later, 12 of those first 17 airplanes were airborne for the F4U-1's first combat mission.

Guadalcanal had been declared secure only five days before VMF-124's Corsairs arrived. They landed at Henderson Field among Marine and Navy pilots who had endured furious hassles with the formidable Japanese A6M Zeke ever since the airstrip was captured in August. Their F4F Wildcats did not measure up favorably in plane-to-plane encounters and could not deliver uncontested air superiority. It was only through aggressive flying, practiced skill at deflection shooting, and mutual support that they held some level of parity. The Japanese operated out of numerous air bases built out in the New Georgia Island group and farther northwest on Bougainville. When the Japanese mounted large air operations, or when attrition ground down inventory, reinforcements would be shuttled down the slot from the massive Japanese air base at Rabaul on New Britain near the northernmost end of the Solomon chain.

With Guadalcanal secured, the campaign to move up the Solomon chain could begin by neutralizing those airfields as Allied forces advanced. The Marine air arm was identified as a vital component in that thrust, and Marine fighter squadrons would spearhead the drive as escorts for bombers and top cover for amphibious

VMF-124

First to deploy and first into combat with the Corsair, members of Marine fighter squadron VMF-124 acquitted themselves well. Formed in September 1942, the squadron received its new F4U-1s in late October and arrived on Guadalcanal on the morning of 12 February 1943. That afternoon, the squadron logged its first combat mission escorting a PBY Catalina on a rescue mission for downed pilots.

A deciding factor in the success of that first deployment was the leadership of squadron commanding officer Major William E. Gise. Never losing sight of the enabling role the Corsair would play in the Solomons, he devoted equal attention to the mechanical shortcomings of the early production F4U-1, the berthing and feeding of the squadron—as challenging as that was in those early days at Guadalcanal—and the thoughtful selection of his most skilled pilots for positions of leadership as division and section leaders. Major Gise deserves credit for establishing the earliest tactical procedures under combat conditions for the Corsair. He devised the protocols for intercept, bomber escort, and fighter sweep that would form the template for Corsair squadrons that followed. Gise would not survive the second squadron deployment into theater; he was killed in action in May 1943.

In three deployments to the southwest Pacific that ended in September 1943, VMF-124 Marines downed 68 Japanese aircraft at a loss of 11 Corsairs in combat. The squadron produced three aces in that time; among them was Lieutenant Ken Walsh, with 20 victories and the presentation of the Medal of Honor.

The squadron returned to the western Pacific in December 1944 under new commanding officer Major William Millington. He led VMF-124, now with F4U-1Ds, aboard USS *Essex* as the first of two Marine fighter squadrons to deploy on big deck carriers. The two squadrons, in operations off the Philippines, Saigon, and in the South China Sea, achieved 10 enemy planes downed and 16 more destroyed on the ground before the Marines were replaced by Navy Corsair squadrons.

(above) VMF-124 squadron pilots kept score on surveyed propeller blades. In this photo, likely taken in late summer 1943, Lieutenant Ken Walsh, by this time a double ace, is seated in the front row centered between the propeller blades. (Kenneth A. Walsh Collection, USMC History Division)

(left) VMF-124 squadron insignia (USMC History Division)

landings. But the diminutive Wildcats simply did not have the range and endurance to stay with the bombers and challenge the Zekes in extended aerial engagements at longer ranges. With the arrival of the Corsair, the calculus changed. The Corsairs could not only escort on longer missions up the slot but also now offer a capable challenge to the Zeke.

Two days after arriving, VMF-124's first aerial combat was a harsh reminder that the Japanese still possessed a formidable air capability in the Solomons. VMF-124's Corsairs escorted B-24s to Bougainville, along with U.S. Army Air Forces P-38s flying high cover and P-40s the low cover. The Japanese were waiting with an estimated 50 Zekes. The outcome was two Zekes shot down for a loss of two P-40s, four P-38s, and two Corsairs. Moving the Solomons campaign forward would mean reducing the heavily fortified Japanese base at Rabaul. Japanese air bases standing along the path to Rabaul had to be rendered ineffective and then remade as Allied air bases. That meant pummeling Japanese air bases in the New Georgia Islands—Segi, Munda, Ondonga, Vila on Kolombangara, and Barakoma on Vella Lavella—and stepping off from there to neutralize air bases on Bougainville—Kahili, Ballale, Buka, and Bunis. Bougainville's proximity to Rabaul would then permit concentrated air assault on Rabaul itself. Harassing air attacks from any and all of these bases in the meantime were a constant threat and had to be neutralized.

BATTER UP: KEN WALSH BEGINS HIS RUN

The first daylight bombing raid on Kahili on Bougainville from Guadalcanal was escorted by VMF-124. This would have been just beyond the extreme end of the F4F Wildcat's escort radius and was only effectively possible now for VMF-124's Corsairs. Then, on 1 April as recorded in Lieutenant Ken Walsh's log, the squadron flew a routine combat air patrol over the nearby Russell Islands. In what would be his first combat in the Corsair, Walsh led six other F4U-1s. When relieved by six U.S. Army Air Forces P-38s, Walsh eased the throttle, downshifted the blowers of his R-2800 engine, and started a gradual descent to guide the formation back to Henderson Field. Excited chatter on the radio alerted him to the fact that the P-38s had flown into a melee, badly outnumbered by an estimated 25 Zekes. Walsh "pressed the throat mic, barked commands with no formality: 'This is Red One, bandits at ten o'clock high . . . prepare to intercept—Mixture rich—Combat power—Gun switches on—Gunsight on—Switch to main tank . . . Out'!"[7] Coming out of a 180-degree turn, he picked up the P-38s and Zekes intermingled in a Lufbery circle. The dogfight was now at twelve o'clock, a few thousand feet above and within a mile of the F4U-1s. One Zeke passed in front of him, but Walsh's wingman had the better lineup and took the shot. Walsh slammed the stick over, and a Japanese Val dive-bomber filled his windscreen. He fired a burst from all six .50-caliber guns and flamed the Val. He recalled thinking that "the power, speed, the rolling ability of this new F4U was tremendous."[8] Pulling up and around, he picked out another Zeke 1,000 feet ahead and below his long nose. The Japanese pilot apparently saw Walsh at the same instant and pulled up into a tight loop. This was the initial move of a deceptive Japanese tactic known as *hineri-komi*, allowing the Japanese pilot to exploit the Zeke's maneuverability at the top of the loop by applying hard left rudder to yaw into a side-slip, then finishing the move with right rudder and opposite aileron to roll to the inside of the tailing aircraft's loop for a deflection shot.[9] This maneuver had worked more

Lieutenant Ken Walsh in his F4U-1 number 13 prior to taxi in September 1943, shortly before VMF-124 was rotated out of the theater. (NARA)

A6M2-21 (Artwork by Dave Douglass)

F4U-1 vs. A6M2-21

	F4U-1 11,194 lbs Full Ammo Engine - P&W R2800-8			**A6M2-21** 5,266 lbs Full Ammo Engine - Nakajima Sakae 12
	Rating*			**Rating****
Power Loading	6.7 lbs/bhp	✓		5.5 lbs/bhp
Wing Loading	35.6 lbs/ft²		✓	22 lbs/ft²
Turn Rate	Using Flaps at > 200 kts, can stay even for ½ turn @ 10,000'		✓	At slow speed, gains one turn in 3½ turns @ 10,000'
Roll Rate	Superior above 250 kts	✓		Equal below 200 kts
Top Speed @ 20k'	378 mph	✓		335 mph
Cockpit Visibility	Birdcage Canopy limits vision - nose obstructs downward vision -	--	--	Birdcage Canopy limits vision, - mitigated by higher seat position -
Lethality of Fire	2 sec. burst = mass of 11 lbs headed down range at target		✓	2 sec. burst = mass of 21 lbs headed down range at target
Vulnerability	• Cockpit armored vs. 7.7mm • Self-sealing fuel tanks	✓		• Lacked self-sealing fuel tanks • Lacked protective pilot armor

Power Loading = Gross Weight ÷ Brake Horsepower / Higher P.L. = better climb rate and faster acceleration

Wing Loading = Gross Weight ÷ Wing Area / Lower W.L. = good instantaneous turn performance and turn rate

Higher Top Speed = maneuvering advantage for faster closure with target, or faster separation from engagement

* C.T. Booth, CDR, USN, "Final Flight Report" of F4U-1 BIS Trials

** René J. Francillon, *Japanese Aircraft of the Pacific War*

(Commander C. T. Booth, USN, "Final Flight Report"; René J. Francillon, *Japanese Aircraft of the Pacific War*)

F4U-1 (Artwork by Chris Busbridge)

often than not against the F4F Wildcat in one-on-one encounters. Walsh was not taken in. Nearing the top of the loop, he rolled the Corsair inverted and pulled through the loop with enough g-force on the airplane to momentarily pull the Zeke into a shooting position, framed in the center of his gunsight reticle. All six .50-caliber guns fired at once, and as he passed close aboard Walsh could see the Zeke's left wing beginning to smoke and then watched it explode as he looked back over his wing.

Walsh noted that in this, his first aerial combat in the Corsair, he scored a Val and two Zeke shootdowns in the first five minutes of contact. He had his own canopy blown off, but the Corsair's armor plating behind the cockpit prevented the round from striking his head. As a whole, VMF-124 with its F4U-1s added seven more aerial victories that same day.[10] Two weeks later, Walsh added two more shootdowns to the record, making him the first Corsair ace. By August, Walsh had run his personal score up to 20.

VMF-124 was joined by more Marine Corsair squadrons as 1943 wore on: VMF-213 (11 March), VMF-121 (15 April), VMF-112 and VMF-221 (19 May), VMF-122 (16 June), VMF-214 (19 June), and VMF-123 (2 July). VMF-124 completed its first deployment and returned to Miramar, California, in October 1943. In its eight months in the Solomons as the first F4U-1 squadron to see combat, the squadron was credited with 68 Japanese aircraft destroyed for 11 Corsairs downed in combat and three pilots lost—a better than 6:1 exchange rate.[11] In the intensely competitive months of August to November 1942, before the appearance of VMF-124's F4Us at Guadalcanal, Marine and Navy land-based F4F Wildcats struggled with the loss of 96 Wildcats in exchange for a claimed 264 Japanese fighters.[12] That measure equated to an exchange rate of 2.75:1, still respectable if accurate but not nearly the war-winning exchange rates that would materialize once the Corsairs appeared. Navy land-based Wildcats during that time added little better than a 1:1 exchange rate with Japanese fighters.[13] As early as 1943, the skill level of Japanese pilots had begun to show a significant decline from the first months of Guadalcanal combat. Equally proficient replacements were simply not available to backfill the first rank of skilled Japanese fighter pilots lost in the Guadalcanal campaign. Yet the scoreboard pointed to an essential altering of the balance with the arrival of the F4U-1 Corsair.

Major Gregory Boyington leans on the empennage of his F4U-1. (NARA)

"BLACK SHEEP" LEADER

Among the F4U-1 squadrons and pilots arriving soon after VMF-124, a brash, charismatic personality appeared in Major Greg Boyington commanding the VMF-214 "Black Sheep." Operating from Munda beginning in September, VMF-214's first opposed mission on 16 September was flying top cover for Marine SBD and TBF bombers on their way to Ballale just south of Bougainville. With Corsairs, bombers, New Zealand P-40s, and a newly arrived contingent of Navy F6Fs—some of the first Hellcats to reach the Solomons—the flight numbered well over 100 aircraft.

Major Boyington (crouching at left) gathers VMF-214 pilots for a pre-mission discussion. (Smithsonian National Air and Space Museum Archives)

Boyington led the formation west around Shortland Island, then turned east so that the flight approached the airfield from out of the afternoon sun. He did not initially see the 30 to 40 Zekes that jumped the formation from behind high cirrus clouds. By his recollection, he was either lulled by the monotony of herding such a large formation or simply had had too much to drink the night before. Boyington suddenly broke left when he saw tracers zipping by his canopy. As the Zeke overshot and pulled back to track Boyington, his VMF-214 wingman pulled behind the Zeke and triggered a burst that was dead on. An A6M3 Zeke pulled ahead and, mistaking Boyington for a wingman, wagged his wings to signal a join-up. Boyington finally charged his guns and tapped his rudder for better lineup of his gunsight. A long burst of his six .50-caliber guns sent the damaged Zeke on a straight-in dive to the water.

Boyington lost sight of his wingman but joined on two other Corsairs—only to realize minutes later they were nowhere to be seen. Zekes were bracketing his airplane again, and he zoomed up into cloud cover. Emerging from the clouds, he saw that his pursuers were gone, but below him he could see the bombers leaving the target area with other Zekes on their tails. He pushed over into a dive, pulled out behind one of the A6Ms, and "opened fire at three hundred yards, the optimum bore-sighting distance for the Corsair's six guns, but his speed differential was so great that in seconds he had closed to fifty feet. At that moment the enemy fighter burst apart. . . . He was fortunate to miss the engine and its still-spinning propeller, but collected numerous dents on his cowling and leading edges of wings and tail surfaces."[14]

Boyington rejoined the bombers on their way home, when his scan caught a Zeke passing through their formation from above. Boyington dived to intercept with a deflection shot as the Zeke pulled up, bleeding off some of his energy. At the top of his loop the Zeke slowed, presenting an easier target for an angle-of-deflection shot that was still very high. Boyington held the trigger down and watched the Zeke disintegrate in a blooming arc of orange flame and black smoke. He climbed to rejoin the formation on its way home when he made out a flight of Zekes returning to Ballale.

He singled out the tailing Zeke in the formation for a high side run, but the pilot saw him coming and entered a very gentle banking turn. Boyington suspected a setup, coordinated to lull him into a wingman's sights. Looking right, then left, he saw the wingman holding back, waiting for him to commit. The Marine pulled his big Corsair around and, from nose-on with the Zeke at 300 yards and closing, held the trigger down. Shards of metal flew off the Zeke's cowling, and it started trailing a thin wisp of gray smoke. Boyington pulled into a hard climbing turn to take the same heading from a high perch, looking down as the Zeke plunged into the ocean. Thinking that was the finale for the day's combat, Boyington started his climb once more. As he passed 10,000 feet, two more Zekes flashed by on their way back to Ballale. He pulled hard into the turn to engage, just as the Zekes started their turn back to come after him. The first Zeke pulled up and right as Boyington flew past him, firing at the wingman. Neither Zeke pressed the attack, nosing over to bug out. Boyington remained at 10,000 feet and, nearing Vella Lavella, scanned a lone Corsair just above the wave tops with two Zekes in hot pursuit. He did a split-S to pull out behind the Zekes and started firing at long range. Seeing they were taking fire, one Zeke began a climbing turn. Boyington pursued and fired a short burst, whereupon the Zeke streamed black smoke and made a gradual sloping descent into the sea. The other was nowhere to be seen. Finally, landing at Munda, Boyington had 10 gallons of fuel remaining and 30 rounds of .50-caliber ammunition unspent.[15] The end of the Black Sheep's first day of combat yielded 11 aerial victories. Of those, Boyington claimed five. If the count was accurate, that made Boyington the first Marine to down five enemy aircraft in a single flight in a Corsair.

CORSAIRS PROLIFERATE

Corsair squadrons were added at a brisk pace throughout 1943, such that at least eight were forward-deployed by the fall. The first Corsair squadron to arrive in theater, VMF-124, was allowed a respite in June 1943 when VMF-213 arrived to relieve it. The replacement's immediate task was to cover landings on New Georgia. Those landings yielded newly captured airfields Barakoma, Ondonga, and Munda. VMF-213 could then shuttle from Guadalcanal to Munda to provide escort for strikes going farther north to Bougainville as summer eased into fall. Their experience was not unlike the other arriving Marine Corsair squadrons in finding plentiful and vigorous opposition in the air. By the end of their tour in December, VMF-213's count totaled 105 Japanese aircraft downed, with 7 aces and 3 of those at least double aces.[16]

VMF-213 commanding officer Major Greg Weissenberger mounts his F4U-1 at Fighter One airstrip on Guadalcanal. VMF-213 relieved VMF-124, the first Marine Corsair squadron to arrive in the Southwest Pacific theater. Both squadrons would later deploy together as part of the USS *Essex* (CV-9) air group. (National Museum of the United States Navy)

KIWI CORSAIRS

When Lieutenant Commander Blackburn arrived with VF-17 at Ondonga airfield on New Georgia in October 1943, his squadron shared ramp space with two Royal New Zealand Air Force (RNZAF) P-40 Kittyhawk squadrons. Three more Kiwi P-40 units arrived within the month. New Zealanders and their P-40s joined U.S. Navy and Marine Corsairs escorting bombers to Bougainville and beyond, demonstrating great skill and daring in air-to-air engagements with the Japanese. Their performance was persuasive.

The British Commonwealth countries with which Britain had the closest relationships—Canada, Australia, and New Zealand—all provided pilots that were incorporated into the Fleet Air Arm. Many would fly Corsairs from Royal Navy aircraft carriers. Yet each country was a signatory to the Empire Air Training Plan, which stipulated that, pending access to adequate equipment, Dominion pilots would serve with units of their own air forces wherever possible. New Zealand's squadrons in the South Pacific operated under a multinational command structure that found them assigned to commander, Air South Pacific Area, and administratively reporting to the U.S. Navy. When their P-40s approached obsolescence on the battlefield, their replacement became the business of the Navy. Under the terms of a mutual aid agreement between the United States and New Zealand signed in September 1942, the Kiwis received 424 Corsairs, more than half of which were F4U-1s. The balance comprised 127 F4U-1Ds and 60 FG-1Ds.

F4U-1 Corsairs of 26 Squadron Royal New Zealand Air Force in flight in 1945. (Northrop Grumman Corporation and Smithsonian National Air and Space Museum Archives)

The first 30 F4U-1s were delivered by USS *Kadashan* (CVE-76) by March 1944 to an RNZAF-operated facility on Espiritu Santo. Once sufficient aircraft had been assembled and flight-tested by a Corsair servicing party, they were delivered to six forward-based Kiwi squadrons. Thereafter, aircraft deliveries were rerouted to an assembly depot at Auckland, New Zealand, to form a pool of ready spares for conversion training and attrition replacement.

Lacking adequate personnel to fully staff every squadron, the squadrons were assigned to one of ten servicing units distributed geographically throughout the theater. These units performed all maintenance, servicing, test-flying, and allocation of aircraft. In practice, the squadrons operated more as extensions of the servicing units. By 1945 13 squadrons were operating F4Us where one or more squadrons would be tethered to the servicing unit depending on their deployment site. Those 13 squadrons rotated in and out of the theater individually after 3 months on the line, normally leaving a maximum of 8 squadrons with 18 aircraft each in the forward area at any one time.

F4U-1Ds for New Zealand began arriving in the theater in June 1944, the same month that the P-40s flew their last operational mission. Far better suited for the ground attack role, the F4U-1Ds were put to good use. At year's end, U.S. units began withdrawing from bases in the Solomon Islands for campaigning closer to the Philippines. Air opposition from the Japanese had in the main been eradicated. Royal Australian Air Force back-filled for the U.S. presence, flying a combination of Boomerangs and Wirraways. The Aussies frequently paired with the Kiwis as spotters to lead the Corsairs in for ground attack runs. The Corsairs' work consisted

primarily of reducing bypassed Japanese garrisons, which still offered vigorous resistance to air attack. Kiwi Corsairs suffered 19 pilots killed in action, with another 33 lost to operational accidents.

At war's end, the British requested that one Kiwi fighter squadron remain in Japan as part of the Allied occupation. RNZAF Squadron No. 14 fulfilled this assignment with its F4U-1Ds, after having completed seven combat deployments in the South Pacific. U.S. policy regarding the disposition of lend-lease Corsairs was resolved by an agreement in July 1946 that New Zealand would not be required to make any payments to settle accounts for the F4Us received during the war. New Zealand assumed title to its Corsairs, but its postwar obligation to the British Commonwealth required that the Corsairs retire, to be replaced by Mosquito fighter-bombers in a "buy British" push.[17]

NOTES

1. Kenneth A. Walsh, "U.S. Marine Aviation in World War II: VMF-124 in the Solomons," interview by Jeffrey Kwallek, Research Report 88-1515 (Maxwell Air Force Base, AL: Air Command and Staff College), https://apps.dtic.mil/sti/pdfs/ADA192519.pdf, 51.

2. LCDR Robert Dosé, USN, cited in Barrett Tillman, *Corsair* (Annapolis, MD: Naval Institute Press, 1979), 13.

3. Carrier Qualification Unit Glenview, "Action Message #1831," 5 April 1943, Record Group 38, National Archives and Records Administration, College Park, MD.

4. Tom Blackburn, *The Jolly Rogers* (Pacifica, CA: Pacifica Press, 1997), 45.

5. Blackburn, *The Jolly Rogers*, 75.

6. John H. Towers, "Action Message #180022," 19 August 1943, Record Group 38, National Archives and Records Administration, College Park, MD.

7. Guyton, *Whistling Death*, 3.

8. Guyton, *Whistling Death*, 4.

9. Mark R. Peattie, *Sunburst* (Annapolis, MD: Naval Institute Press, 2001), 183.

10. Robert Sherrod, *History of Marine Corps Aviation in World War II* (Washington, DC: Combat Forces Press, 1952), 137.

11. Sherrod, *History of Marine Corps Aviation*, 135.

12. Stuart B. Barber, *Naval Aviation Combat Statistics World War II*, OPNAV-P- 23V No. A129 (Washington, DC: Air Branch, Office of Naval Intelligence, Office of the Chief of Naval Operations, 17 June 1946).

13. John Lundstrom, *The First Team and the Guadalcanal Campaign* (Annapolis, MD: Naval Institute Press, 1994), 528.

14. Bruce Gamble, *Black Sheep One* (New York: Random House, 2000), 270.

15. Gamble, *Black Sheep One*, 273.

16. Barrett Tillman, *U.S. Marine Corps Fighter Squadrons of World War II* (Oxford: Osprey Publishing, 2014), 104.

17. Robert E. Montgomery, *Pacific Corsair* (Wellington, NZ: Venture Publications, 2023), 96.

NAVY CORSAIRS ENTER COMBAT

From *Lexington* days, I knew Blackburn's precision method, tight above the runway—like the carrier's deck, roll one airplane after the other close behind the leader, and land in exact intervals. Mission complete.

—Boone Guyton[1]

Two F4U-2 night-fighter Corsairs of VF(N)-101 position for launch on the flight deck of USS *Enterprise* in the spring of 1944. Commanded by Lieutenant Commander Richard E. Harmer, VF(N)-101 was split off from the original night-fighter unit VF(N)-75 that saw action in the Solomons earlier in the war. During its time on *Enterprise*, VF(N)-101 would tally ten night intercepts, resulting in five enemy bombers shot down, two more probably destroyed, and two damaged. (Smithsonian National Air and Space Museum)

LAUNCH THE "BAT"!

Despite Tom Blackburn's determination to get his Corsairs into action first, VF-17 would not be alone as the initial Navy F4U squadron to see combat. A Corsair night-fighting squadron, VF(N)-75, shared that distinction. The story of the night-capable F4U-2 began in January 1942, fully five months before the first production F4U-1 flew, and at a moment when the Corsair's handling issues around the ship were still clouded. That month the Navy reviewed a mock-up that Vought had constructed with an assist from the Sperry Gyroscope Company and the Massachusetts Institute of Technology Radiation Laboratory. It was apparent to all in January 1942 that Vought was flush with F4U-1 production work and could not bear the distraction of a one-off development and production effort. So BuAer assigned further radar system development and testing to the Naval Air Station at Quonset Point, Rhode Island, with actual modification of the F4U-1 into the F4U-2 accomplished at the Naval Aircraft Factory at Philadelphia. Thirty-four night-fighters were produced as modified F4U-1s. Two more were later modified in the field by night-fighting squadron VMF(N)-532 on the island of Roi.

The most obvious external alteration to the airplane was the integration of the 18-inch parabolic antenna inside a teardrop-shaped dome faired into the leading edge of the right wing. The antenna transmitted energy from a Sperry AN/APS-4 radar set that broadcast in X-band, the beam in the form of a six-degree cone that the pilot could direct in one of three modes: manual, search, and intercept. On a three-inch radarscope in the center of the instrument panel, the search range scale went out to four miles, but effectiveness diminished for air targets much beyond two miles. The mounting of the antenna dome required removal of the outer .50-caliber gun to restore longitudinal balance in flight. The added electrical power draw required a larger generator, which in turn required a small air scoop on the right-hand side of the fuselage to handle the added cooling load. Finally, flame dampeners were added to mask the heat signature from engine exhaust ports on the underside of the fuselage behind the cowl.[2]

Formed in April 1943, the Navy's first night-fighter squadron, VF(N)-75, received its initial allocation of F4U-2s upon standup. Squadron skipper Lieutenant Commander William "Gus" Widhelm started training with 18 pilots, only 6 of whom had prior experience in fleet fighters. In August, he took his 6 best pilots and 11 enlisted men, with the squadron's F4U-2s, to their new home in the Solomons, with directions to eliminate the nightly nuisance overflights by Japanese aircraft. After acclimating to night operations in the area, the squadron flew its first mission from Munda on 2 October. The squadron achieved its first kill in the early morning hours of 1 November when Lieutenant Hugh O'Neil was vectored to a position behind a Japanese G4M Betty bomber, bringing it down off Vella Lavella.[3] Although night-fighting tactics were still raw and electronics were temperamental, VF(N)-75 claimed five more Japanese planes shot down over the next four months.[4]

ON DECK: THE "JOLLY ROGERS"

Blackburn led the Jolly Rogers, 34 F4U-1As, into the break over Ondonga airfield on 27 October 1943 by divisions in echelons of four. The single runway, composed of crushed coral and Marston matting, had been completed by Navy Seabees only weeks before. Reclaimed from dense jungle on the far western extension of New Georgia Island, it now served as the next advanced base up the Solomons chain for strikes on Bougainville and beyond by VF-17's Corsairs alongside Marine F4U, SBD, and PBJ units, as well as an Army Air Force P-39 detachment. Navy Corsairs of VF-17 flew into their first opposed mission from Ondonga three days later on 1 November. Assigned top cover for Allied landings at Torokina on Bougainville, VF-17's eight Corsairs orbited ten miles northwest of the landing operation at 25,000 feet. Unbeknownst to Blackburn's squadron, complete air groups from three Japanese carriers (*Shokaku*, *Zuikaku*, and *Zuiho*), temporarily land-based at Rabaul, were inbound to break up the landings. These units, fresh from carrier duty, injected a level of skill and experience for the Japanese that had atrophied over months of combat in the Solomons.

Blackburn recalled the engagement this way:

> I immediately sighted a good-sized formation about 15 miles to the east-northeast and about 10,000 feet below. They were heading directly toward the landing area. I fired a short burst to alert the flight, bent on full combat power, took

> a heading to intercept, and tried to convey by sign language that we were going in on an attack. First combat! The tension and concentration were almost corporeal. The targets were eighteen Val dive-bombers at 14,000 feet escorted by a dozen Zeke [A6M Zeke] fighters at 16,000 feet. We flew into the Japanese formation from five o'clock at a shallow dive angle, indicating 350 knots. I set up to shoot at the fighter leader. When I was 1,000 yards from my prey, all the Zekes dropped their belly tanks. Instantly, the leader, followed in quick succession by his three wingmen, honked his Zeke around in a tight, tight right climbing turn. I opened fire at 500 yards and held the trigger down until I had to flick the Big Hog's nose up to clear him. I am sure I got rounds into him, but did not nail him. I suddenly found myself coming up fast on the tail of a Zeke, holding fire until he filled my windscreen. The next thing I knew, I was flying through a fireball, emerging with a coating of oil and hydraulic fluid. Wow! What a sensation![5]

The Jolly Rogers skipper scored one more Zeke shootdown to add two to the squadron's tally of five with no Corsairs lost. Three more Corsair flights of eight airplanes each sortied later that day, producing two more victories for the loss of one pilot and his F4U. As Blackburn recalled, it was not the squadron's absolute best day, but it was a day that taught several lessons. First, the Japanese were quick to spot and attack singles, so section (two aircraft) and division (four aircraft) formation integrity was essential. Second, radio silence was not helpful to situation awareness, and section leaders should broadcast continuously what they were seeing up until the engagement. Finally, Blackburn and his pilots were exposed to the Japanese vertical scissors maneuver for the first time; it taught that using the second section of Corsairs to engage the lead target's wingman effectively broke up the maneuver.

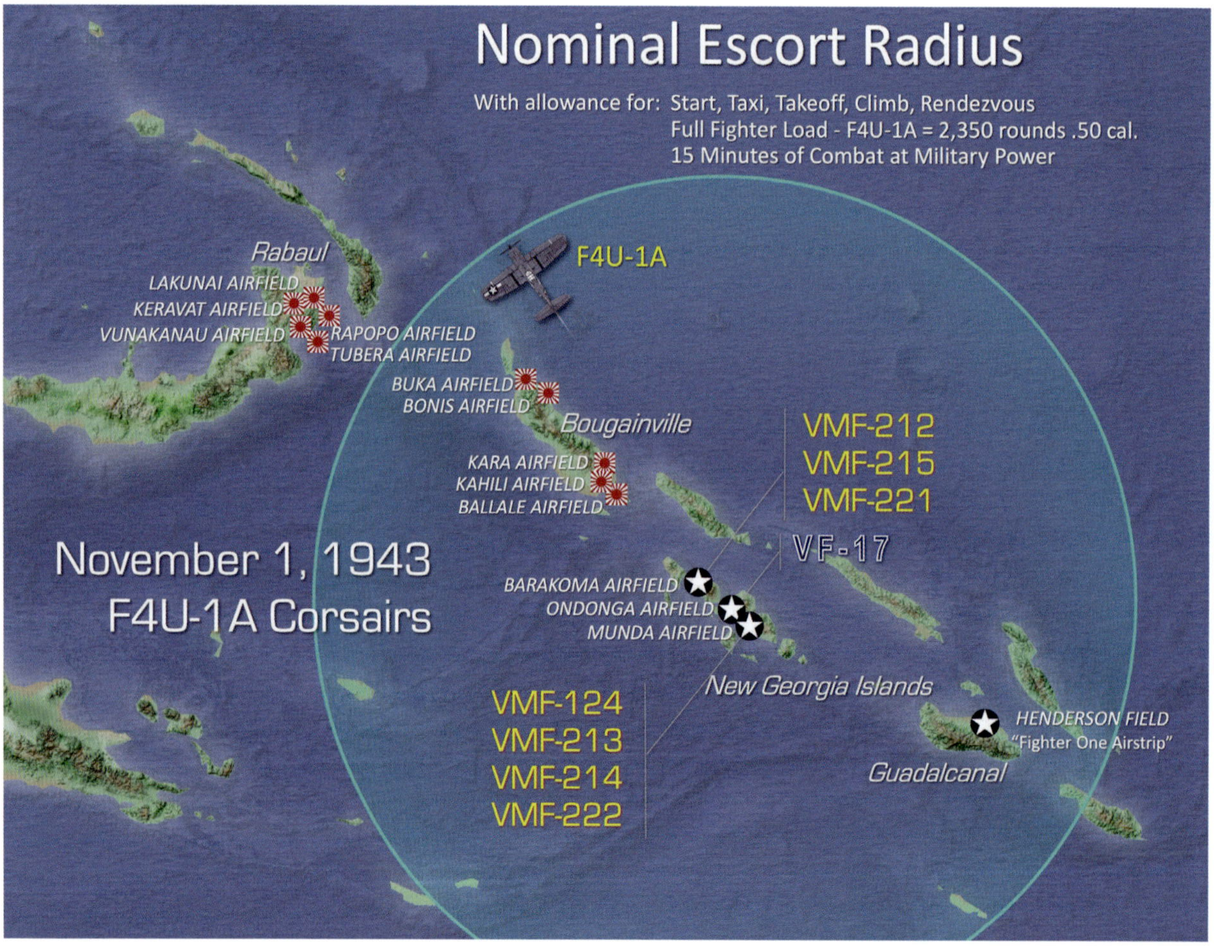

As Allied operations moved up the Solomons chain, more Corsair squadrons began arriving on newly captured airfields Barakoma, Munda, and Ondonga. Marine squadrons were joined by the first Navy Corsair squadron to deploy at Ondonga airfield on New Georgia in November 1943. Corsairs now could escort strike missions on enemy airfields and fortifications throughout Bougainville. (Artwork by Aldo Spadoni)

A formation of VF-17 Corsairs flies over Bougainville in March 1944. Number 29 is flown by Lieutenant (junior grade) Ira "Ike" Kepford, then the Navy's leading ace with 16 kills. The pilot of plane number 8 is Lieutenant (junior grade) Earl May, who would soon achieve ace status. Corsair number 3 is flown by Ensign Frederick "Jim" Streig, already an ace, and number 28 is flown by Ensign Wilbert "Beads" Popp. (NHHC)

Lieutenant Commander Tom Blackburn stands confidently in front of VF-17's scoreboard in February 1944. (NARA)

Lieutenant Commander Tom Blackburn and VF-17

Tom Blackburn was teaching gunnery at Opa-Locka, Florida, when news broke of the attack on Pearl Harbor. He was ordered to take command of Escort Fighting Squadron 29 (VGF-29) flying Grumman F4Fs. The squadron entered action against Vichy forces in Operation Torch near Casablanca, Morocco. It was a humbling experience. On his first mission, he led four other F4Fs back to USS *Santee*, not realizing the ship's hayrake antenna system had malfunctioned. Lost over a cloud deck, he ordered his flight back to shore, where they were taken captive by Vichy troops. Blackburn ran out of fuel and ditched. Floating in ten-foot swells for three days, he was finally spotted and rescued by a task force destroyer.

A 1933 graduate of the Naval Academy, Blackburn was a stand-out water polo swimmer for the midshipmen but would evince an assured confidence in the air only in time. He proved to be an exceptional combat leader in the Pacific.

Blackburn was assigned command of VF-17, a squadron selected for transition to the new F4U-1 Corsair. A fierce advocate for the airplane and his pilots, he insisted on tight tactical discipline in the air. He would not brook reports of "probables," accepting reports only of kills. Under Blackburn's command, VF-17, in 76 combat days, racked up a confirmed kill score of 154.5 Japanese airplanes with a kill-to-loss ratio better than 11:1. Thirteen VF-17 pilots made ace in that period—an unbeaten combat record throughout the war for a single Corsair squadron.

In May 1944, VF-17 reformed as an F6F squadron, its F4U-1As left behind at Espiritu Santo, its pilots returned to Pearl Harbor for reassignment. They were treated to the "party to end all parties" at the Mark Hopkins Hotel in San Francisco, hosted by plane maker Chance Vought. Eight pilots went on to populate new Corsair squadrons, VF-84 in *Bunker Hill*, and VF-10 or VBF-10 in *Intrepid*. All eight would again fly Corsairs in action at Okinawa.

CARRIER COMPATIBILITY AFFIRMED

Ten days later, VF-17 flew its most consequential mission in terms of reshaping perceptions about the Corsair's "sea legs." It started with plans to avert a Japanese surface attack on the Torokina invasion force by preemptively attacking Japanese ships and airfields at Rabaul. This was an all-out effort that involved air groups from USS *Essex*, USS *Bunker Hill*, and USS *Independence* in the attack on shipping, augmented by air group strikes from USS *Saratoga* and USS *Princeton* to the north. The carrier air groups' Hellcat fighters were to escort their air carrier air group attackers to the target while land-based fighter squadrons were to fly top cover for the carriers. Blackburn got the call for VF-17 to provide that top cover with 24 airplanes, along with a land-based F6F squadron, VF-33. When the F4U-1A and F6F-3 on combat air patrol reached low fuel states, they were to recover on the carriers for refueling and rearming, replaced overhead by 32 more Corsairs from land-based VMF-212 and VMF-221 and a New Zealand P-40 outfit. When serviced and readied by the flight deck crews on the carriers, VF-17's Corsairs and VF-33's Hellcats would launch and resume station over the carrier task group, relieving the Marine F4Us for return to base.

In the mission prebrief session at Munda, Commander, Aircraft Solomons Major General Nathan Twining turned to Blackburn and inquired with an air of skepticism: "The word we have is that you were sent down here because the F4U isn't carrier suitable. Can you handle it?" Blackburn was unreservedly direct: "General, that story that our Corsairs aren't carrier suitable is hogwash. My guys cut their teeth at carrier work with the old F4Us on a little bitty slow escort carrier. An *Essex*-class ship with plenty of wind over the deck is a piece of cake. Every landing approach we make [at Ondonga airfield] is a simulated carrier pass. My people are good! It'll be no sweat, sir."[6]

Lieutenant (junior grade) Ike Kepford taxis Corsair number 29 to join a fighter sweep over Rabaul in February 1944. (NARA)

The squadron had a day to prepare, which meant reattaching tailhooks that had been removed to lighten aircraft weight. On 11 November 1943 reveille was at two o'clock in the morning, followed by takeoff at four o'clock. Blackburn led six divisions of VF-17 Corsairs in a formation of 23 airplanes. Overhead the carriers in the early morning light, one snooper flight by a probing Japanese Ki-61 Tony was intercepted and dispatched. With the arrival of the Marine F4Us, VF-17 split into two flights. Blackburn took his 11 toward *Bunker Hill*, and his executive officer, Lieutenant Roger Hedrick, took 18 Corsairs toward *Essex*. In Blackburn's words: "Fighting-17 provided textbook perfect landings—good tight intervals, no wave-offs, no hairy passes, no blown tires. . . . If ever there was a question about the Corsair's suitability for carrier ops we laid it to rest that morning."[7]

Carrier air groups returning later that morning dragged behind them the expected counterstrike from the Japanese air groups—dozens of Zekes and Vals. Blackburn's squadron was by then on station and ready. In the ensuing melee, the Jolly Rogers took down 18.5 confirmed kills for the loss of one Corsair, with that pilot ultimately rescued. Not yet evident to Blackburn and his squadron was the significance of that day's operation. There would be hard fighting to come, but the Japanese now recognized their strategic position at Rabaul was greatly weakened and untenable. With air bases at Torokina and Buka on Bougainville coming into Allied possession, land-based bombers and fighters could finish the business of pacifying Rabaul. Corsairs in particular could provide the range and staying power over Rabaul to protect the bombers and join in on strafing ground targets when the bombers were clear.

The Jolly Rogers moved up to fighter strip Piva Yoke at Torokina in January 1944 to join the 17 Corsairs of VMF-216 and the night-fighting F4U-2s of VF(N)-75, up from Munda. A change in Japanese tactics soon became evident. To conserve their diminished fighter force at Rabaul, they would not respond to massed Allied fighter sweeps, instead only coming up to attack Allied bomber formations, singling out and overwhelming the Allied escort fighters. This was maddeningly apparent to Lieutenant Colonel Greg Boyington leading a large fighter sweep of Corsairs over Rabaul, which, when taunting Japanese fighters by radio to come up and engage, was rebuffed as they waited for easier targets to appear. Blackburn's VF-17 pilots devised a countertactic that they coined roving high cover. Additional Corsairs would be assigned to fly well over and ahead of escorted bomber formations to take on Japanese intercepts. In late January, a first test of the tactic proved exceptionally productive in a strike on Tobera airfield in East New Britain south of Rabaul. What was planned as a roving high cover formation of four Corsairs was reduced in flight by mechanical gripes to two, led by Lieutenant (junior grade) Ike Kepford. Kepford by this time was a high scorer in VF-17 with six confirmed kills. Approaching the target, they spotted a dozen Zekes below them headed for the strike formation and dived into the attack immediately. "Trading the lead after each firing run, the two maintained perfect cohesion in one textbook attack after another. In ten minutes of continuous high-side and overhead firing passes, with sharp chandelles in between, they accounted for four Zekes apiece."[8]

On the next roving high cover mission, Kepford pulled up from an attack at just 1,000 feet to see three Zekes in line abreast bearing down him. He "was flying one of the squadron's eight Corsairs that had been retrofitted in Espiritu Santo with Pratt & Whitney's new water injection system. He wound the engine up to 2,750 rpm and 62 inches of manifold pressure. There were few aircraft in the world that could match that performance."[9] The surge of power-on-demand obtainable with water injection in the R-2800–8W gave Kepford enough speed advantage in level flight to easily extricate himself from an unfavorable situation.

NOTES

1. Guyton, *Whistling Death*, 220.

2. Bert Kinzey, *F4U Corsair in Detail & Scale, Part 1: XF4U Through F2G* (Carrollton, TX: Squadron/Signal, 1998), 63.

3. William C. Odell, "The Development of Night Fighters in World War II," *Naval History Magazine* 3, no. 1 (January 1989), https://www.usni.org/magazines/naval-history-magazine/1989/january/development-night-fighters-world-war-ii.

4. Sherrod, *History of Marine Corps Aviation*, 167.

5. Blackburn, *The Jolly Rogers*, 131.

6. Blackburn, *The Jolly Rogers*, 135.

7. Blackburn, *The Jolly Rogers*, 204.

8. Blackburn, *The Jolly Rogers*, 243.

9. Blackburn, *The Jolly Rogers*, 243.

SUITABILITY QUESTIONED (AGAIN)

> In the end, Lindbergh considered the F4U the "best Navy fighter" built during the war.
>
> — A. Scott Berg, *Lindbergh*[1]

The first F4U-1D to roll off the Vought assembly line (Bureau Number 50050) in April 1944 was accepted later that month by the Navy. After trial landings with -1D models by VF-301 on USS *Gambier Bay* (CVE-73), the F4U-D was cleared for carrier basing. Vought manufactured 1,685 F4U-1D models, *Goodyear* another 2,019 FG-1Ds, and Brewster eked out 179 F3A-1Ds, the last variant produced before Brewster's demise as prime manufacturer. (NARA)

CARRIER SUITABILITY (FINALLY) PUT TO REST

Despite real-world evidence to the contrary, amply demonstrated by VF-17 on 11 November 1943, a reputation for poor carrier approach handling traits persisted. Not only had VF-17 shown that it was possible to operate the Corsair from carrier decks, but F4U-2 night-fighters returned to carrier basing as a part of a regular Air Group 10 deployment on USS *Enterprise* (CV-6) in January 1944. Reporting to *Enterprise*, the four-plane, four-pilot unit was equipped with airplanes that had not yet received fixes for the wing drop or the hard bouncing oleo. Making things more difficult, most landings were at night in a darkened ship condition. The fleet remained skeptical. Yet the night-fighters' disruption to regular flight deck routine by working well into the early hours of the morning was overlooked when understood that they were reducing snoopers and nighttime torpedo attacks.

The resistance to Corsairs operating on carriers came to a head in March 1944, and it had mostly to do with student experience in the carrier-landing phase of their training. The chief of naval air operational training at Jacksonville, Florida, drafted a letter recommending that Corsairs be restricted from carrier operations. The Corsair bounce had not yet been corrected on the airplanes he was seeing, and student attrition was unusually high. Had the letter been transmitted, Corsairs would probably have never seen carrier duty and would have faded into obscurity as a World War II footnote. Captain John Pearson, fighter design officer in BuAer, and Captain H. S. Duckworth, chief of staff, Fleet Air Jacksonville, were persuasive in holding the letter up until Vought's Russ Clark and his engineering representatives were able to fly in to remedy the problem.

On-scene fixes were made to the landing gear oleos, and assurances were given that the fix was already

A F6F-3 launches from USS *Gambier Bay* (CVE-73) as F4U-1Ds await launch for transition training of new Corsair pilots in late spring 1944. (NARA)

An F4U-1D pilot is waved aboard during transition training. (NARA)

adopted as an engineering change on the production line. Post-fix test flights conducted by Commander T. K. Wright and Lieutenant Colonel John Dobbin validated the efficacy of the fixes. The Corsair won an immediate endorsement from commander, Fleet Air Jacksonville. The assurance was timely, as the first F4U-1D finished post-production test flights at Stratford and was accepted into Navy inventory the next month.

THE DEFINITIVE WARTIME CORSAIR: F4U-1D

The D series update built on the Corsair's already demonstrated prowess as an air-to-air fighter by "exploiting its versatility in handling new combat missions."[2] This simply meant incorporating more firepower that gave the Corsair a punishing ground attack capability. Two pylons were added, one under each stub wing that could support a 1,000-pound bomb or a 154-gallon fuel drop tank. An emerging need dictated that each of these pylons also be made capable of carrying one large 11.75-inch "Tiny Tim" rocket for greater lethality against ships and reinforced pillboxes on land. As a new source for fuel from externally mounted tanks, the pylons permitted removal of the two 63-gallon leading edge tanks in the wings. With room and weight freed up on the wings, tabs or mounts were added for carrying four 5-inch high-velocity aircraft rockets under each wing. And ammunition for the outer two .50-caliber guns could be increased from 375 to 400 rounds per gun.

Beyond D enhancements for more weapons, other changes included addition of the all-bubble, clear-vision canopy that removed the two overhead frames (although more than 800 Ds rolled off the production line before this feature was cut in), and replacement of the propeller with broader, three-inch-shorter blades that produced greater thrust on takeoff with heavy payloads. Also during production of the F4U-1D, a step was cut into the right inboard flap to ease the pilot's climb up to the cockpit. Taken together, these changes culminated in a design that could be truly described as the premier fighter-bomber of World War II.

A distinguishing feature of the F4U-1D was the installation of tabs or mounts—four under each wing—to allow the Corsair to carry 5-inch high-velocity rockets. (NARA)

Changes that made the Corsair into a F4U-1D—or FG-1D for those produced by Goodyear—were incorporated on the production line with negligible impact on the delivery schedule. When the Navy accepted its first F4U-1D on 22 April 1944, the new series Corsairs were rolling off the line at the Stratford factory at the rate of 250 per month. As quickly as ferry flights could be arranged, F4U-1Ds were on their way to the West Coast for transshipment by escort carrier to Marine squadrons in the central Pacific that had been flying F4U-1s or F4U-1As. At least 50 of those early production model F4U-1Ds and FG-1Ds made it to VF-301, -302, and -303 in Los Alamitos as transition trainers for Navy pilots that were assigned to Corsairs in increasing numbers. With the question of carrier suitability seemingly put to rest in most quarters, and with numbers of F4U-1Ds ramping up quickly in Marine and Navy squadrons, the question now at hand for Navy leaders became which airplane to make the standard Navy fighter going forward.

THE CORSAIR AND THE LONE EAGLE

Charles Lindbergh was commissioned by United Aircraft on behalf of Vought to consult with the company on embryonic new designs and to occasionally fill the gap by flying production test flights when the pool of Vought pilots was stretched thin. Beginning in the spring of 1944, after some behind-the-scenes lobbying with senior defense officials for authorization to travel to an active war zone, Lindbergh's consultant duties took him to the central Pacific. His assignment was to obtain feedback from Corsair operators but also to share his expertise with a number of active Marine squadrons in the combat theater. He traded on his reputation as America's foremost aviator to bluff his way into the cockpit with squadrons that still dropped live ordnance on bypassed Japanese island bastions in the rear areas. His zeal to fly on actual missions exposed him on numerous occasions to direct enemy fire, but this, he believed, made him a more authentic and credible spokesman.

One of Lindbergh's first stops was the island of Kwajalein, where he was hosted by Marine Corsair squadron VMF-311. Kwajalein had been envisioned in the early campaigning as a base for future B-29 operations. Before a decision was made to locate B-29 strips elsewhere, Kwajalein's ordnance magazines had been stocked with 2,000-pound bombs. With Kwajalein

Charles Lindbergh (third from left), in his consulting capacity for Vought Aircraft Company on behalf of United Aircraft, visited VMF-223 on the Green Islands in New Guinea, 24 May 1944. With Lindbergh are (left to right) are Edward Firestone, Vincent Lipovsky, and Henry Emery. (Smithsonian National Air and Space Museum Archives)

Lindbergh arrives on the island of Emirau on 25 May 1944, escorted by Major Joe Foss, commanding officer of Corsair squadron VMF-115. Seen between them and slightly behind is Major Marion Carl, commanding officer of Corsair squadron VMF-223 and a leading ace at the time with 18.5 aerial victories. (USMC History Division)

bypassed, those bombs sat idle. Marines and their Corsairs on Kwajalein had been consigned to reducing nearby Japanese bunkers to rubble, and they coveted those 2,000-pounders for the job. Lindbergh added Kwajalein to his itinerary after hearing of VMF-311's efforts to employ those bombs. He fell in with Captain "Fran" Clark, who, with his squadron commander's permission, was trying to field-engineer a means for their Corsairs to upload the 2,000-pound bombs. The two collaborated to improvise a center fuselage bomb rack that could safely carry—and drop—a big payload from a stores station unsanctioned by the current engineering specs or flight manuals. Flightworthiness checks were flown by Lindbergh himself.

By the end of the summer, Lindbergh was spending more time with VMF-115 at Emirau, with occasional excursions to Roi. On the morning of 13 September, he flew his last combat mission with VMF-115 before leaving the theater, a mission that established the upper limits of the Corsair's bombing capability. Five days earlier, and with the squadron skipper's approval, Lindbergh had completed a mission with a 1,000-pound bomb riding on the centerline pylon that adjoined two more 1,000-pound bombs on the stub wing pylons. On this last mission, shuttling from Emirau to Roi to reach targets in Wotje some 150 miles farther east, he carried a 2,000-pound bomb on the centerline along with two 1,000-pound bombs under the stub wings. At 8,000

The 3,608th Corsair, an F4U-1D, was modified in production by Vought to become the F4U-1C. The distinguishing feature of the C was the set of four Hispano M2 20-mm guns, each with 120 rounds, that replaced all six .50-caliber guns in the wings for more hitting power in the air-to-ground role. To prevent any growth in weight, the wing bomb racks were removed. Only 200 C models were produced by Vought, none by Brewster or Goodyear. (NARA)

feet over a small concrete blockhouse on Wotje, he rolled into a 65-degree dive, anticipating a salvo release of all three bombs. In the excitement of the moment, he failed to roll his elevator trim tab far enough forward, making the airplane feel tail-heavy. Without tremendous pressure on the stick, he had difficulty holding the sight on the target. At the moment of release, he found that to drop all three bombs in salvo, he had to pull mechanical levers with his right hand to let the 1,000-pounders go and simultaneously press an electrical-powered bomb release button with his right thumb to release the centerline 2,000-pounder—all while holding excessive forward pressure on the stick to keep the bombsight centered on the target, then immediately pulling back with force to extricate himself from the blast. He missed the blockhouse completely, but by happenstance, his bombs bracketed and eviscerated a large naval gun emplacement, sending a column of smoke and debris several hundred feet into the air.[3]

Lindbergh rightfully deserves credit for demonstrating the F4U-1D's fighter's full range of bombing capability. Even though it is not recorded that this heavy a bomb load was ever again carried operationally, the military utility of fighter and ground attack in a single aircraft would be on display in the Iwo Jima and Okinawa campaigns getting underway six months later.

Coming on the heels of the F4U-1D was a Corsair variant even more highly refined for attack of hardened land targets and ships. Produced only by Vought, the F4U-1C retained many of the features of the F4U-1D, including the two stub wing pylons for 1,000-pounders and the four mounts under each wing for 5-inch rockets. The primary difference from the F4U-1D was that the C swapped its six .50-caliber guns for four Hispano-licensed AN/M2 20-mm cannons. This reduced ammunition to 924 rounds for the four cannons, far less than the 2,400 rounds carried for the six machine guns. Depressing the trigger for one second threw out 11 pounds of projectile mass from the 20-mm guns with all four barrels firing, compared to roughly 7 pounds for the .50-caliber gun with all six barrels firing. That equated to a lot more destructive mass flying downrange. But the difference in rate of fire could well mean more rounds concentrated in a smaller area for the .50-caliber guns, allowing that the pilot could hold the gun-sight pipper on a wildly maneuvering target for only a few seconds at a time. And the .50-caliber guns gave the pilot close to 30 seconds of continuous fire compared to a far briefer 20 seconds of fire for the 20-mm if the trigger were held down, due to the greater amount of ammunition that could be carried for the machine guns. That equated to more time of fire with the .50-caliber to service more targets.

Some pilots generally preferred the higher rate of fire on the chance that they would fight maneuvering aircraft on any given mission—it was generally a matter of personal preference. Given that, most Corsair .50-caliber ammunition was belted in the ratio of one armor piercing, one tracer, one incendiary; "a mere two-second burst of fire would expend approximately 150 rounds—more than enough for a Zero" and sufficient for four to five engagements if judiciously used.[4] The F4U-1D configuration was the starting point for the F4U-1C changes. Once F4U-1D production was up and running, F4U-1Cs would be drawn off the D line for mods in small batches for a total run of 200 aircraft, a forerunner of the later purpose-built AU-1 Corsair. The most conspicuous examples of F4U-1Cs in operational employment came in the spring of 1945 in and around Okinawa.

NOTES

1. A. Scott Berg, *Lindbergh* (New York: Berkley Books, 1999), 455.

2. Guyton, *Whistling Death*, 181.

3. Charles A. Lindbergh, *The Wartime Journals of Charles A. Lindbergh* (New York: Harcourt Brace Jovanovich, 1970), 921.

4. Walsh, interview, 47.

THE BEST NAVY FIGHTER?

> The fighter most wanted to supplement the Hellcat was already well known as a Jap-killer, the "Whistling Death" Corsair.
>
> —Clark G. Reynolds,
> *The Fast Carriers*[1]

THE MYTH OF ZERO INVINCIBILITY

A reliable gauge of the Corsair's combat performance will most often be the perception of the Japanese pilots who encountered it and fought against it. In this, however, opinions vary. One very well-known high-scoring Japanese navy ace, Saburo Sakai, put it this way: "Although most Zero [Zeke] pilots respected the Corsair, they did not fear it. The only time you could really shoot it down was when it was fleeing. You had to shoot it from a certain angle, otherwise the bullets would bounce off. A few times, I would see the F4U making low level diving attacks and dive into a coconut grove or water because it couldn't pull out—the plane was too heavy. We would sometimes chase them into the sea. We didn't have this problem because our planes were so light."[2]

In a more sweeping observation, the designer of the Zeke, Jiro Horikoshi, offered that the Corsair was "the first single-engine fighter to seriously challenge the Zero. . . . In a short period of time the excellent qualities of the Corsair became only too evident, and the enemy rapidly increased the Corsair fighter strength in the Solomons Campaign. . . . Faster than the Zero in level flight and capable of infinitely greater diving speeds, the Corsair soon proved to be a great nuisance to our fighters."[3]

The unexpected recovery of a Zeke from the muskeg in Akutan, Alaska, provided the earliest occasion for head-to-head comparison between the Zeke and the Corsair. In an attack on U.S. Navy facilities at Dutch Harbor in June 1942, the Zeke, an A6M2 Model 21, was damaged by ground fire and crash-landed about 20 miles away, the wheels digging in and tail flipping over as the pilot attempted a gear-down landing in soft mud. Discovered a month later purely by happenstance, the Zeke was hauled out and sent to Naval Air Station North Island, where it was restored to flying condition. Lieutenant Commander Eddie Sanders was delegated from the flight test department at Anacostia to do the early flight test evaluation. In October, Commander Frederick Trapnell, head of flight test, flew one of the Anacostia Corsairs that was then in service out to San Diego for mock dogfights with Sanders in the Zeke: "The Corsair outperformed the Zero in every way except turning radius at low speed, and the difference was more marked in favor of the Corsair as altitude increased over 15,000 feet."[4]

As early as spring 1943, many in the U.S. Navy acknowledged that if the Corsair's carrier landing problems were satisfactorily contained, the service would have two exceptionally good fighters going head-to-head for procurement, training, and support dollars. The need for many thousands of airplanes to carry the war to its logical end tended to mask the duplication for the moment. To get the most from both, BuAer commissioned the two leading fighter contractors to do in-house flight tests to normalize performance comparisons. Grumman was sent one F4U-1A, and Vought received an F6F-3. Grumman's instructions were to familiarize with the F4U-1A's strongest features to discern ways to eke out more speed and maneuvering responsiveness that might be applied to the Hellcat but especially in aileron construction. With the Grumman fighter, Vought's instructions were to examine ways to improve cockpit visibility and internal layout. Grumman found in their assessment that both fighters had almost the same speed at the low and high blower stages from 5,000 feet up to service ceiling but that the Corsair consistently showed a 20-knot airspeed advantage and pulled away inside a few minutes. Grumman reasoned that was due to the Corsair's engine and carburetor getting ram air directly from the forward-facing wing root ducts in main stage blower, whereas the Hellcat's carburetor air came from an accessory compartment behind the engine. The Hellcat was getting carb air at the same pressure as if motionless on the ground, while the Corsair's air was supercharged by the forward speed of

The F4U-1 early production cockpit that Corsair pilots in the Solomons campaign in 1943 would have been familiar with. The relatively uncluttered instrument panel is nearly identical to that of the Grumman F6F-3 in layout of primary flight instruments. On the pilot's left and right, however, the F4U-1 cockpit presented a jumble of switches that could be distracting, especially under the throttle quadrant. Significant improvement in cockpit layout would not appear until introduction of the F4U-4 late in the war. (NARA)

the airplane. And in turn performance, Grumman found the F4U-1A did exceedingly well due to the Corsair's lateral instability when compared to the Hellcat, even after Grumman duplicated a set of molded plywood ailerons for the Hellcat based on the Corsair's aileron shape. Grumman was finally able to reduce stick forces by adopting a NACA-engineered spring tab at the back of their control surface. This would be a standard production modification for their F6F-5. For Vought's part, a hands-on examination of the Hellcat helped in visualizing a production-ready modification that would eventually ease the Corsair's oleo bounce. Cockpit layout could be vastly improved, but those improvements would not appear until the late-war F4U-4 series.[5]

JOINT SERVICE FIGHTER CONFERENCE—JANUARY 1944

Wartime pressures amplified BuAer's intense interest in refining and improving the Navy's fighter designs. This focus soon elevated to a defense-wide examination of comparative fighter performance. In a rare but laudatory display of interservice collaboration, a joint working conference was convened on fighter performance in January 1944. The Army's Fighter and Air Defense Branch of U.S. Army Air Forces headquarters organized an evaluation of the premier Allied fighter aircraft at Eglin Field, Florida, under the auspices of the Proving Ground Command, inviting members of the Navy's BuAer, the Royal Air Force, the Royal Naval Air Service, aircraft designers and test pilots from the producing companies, and pilots from all the military services. The conference was built on an earlier, less comprehensive examination of fighter aircraft characteristics that was held at Eglin in May 1943 but was now expanded to include many of the technological advancements that had appeared in the intervening months. Since the prior conference, aircraft were in production and early delivery to the services that included paddle propellers, water injection, bubble canopies, and improved bomb and auxiliary wing tank shackles, and for the Army Air Forces, two new types that were not available at the earlier conference, the XP-40Q and P-63A.

Two airplanes of each fighter type in the services were flown to Eglin, and ten pilots from the Army Air Forces, four from the Navy, four from the Marine Corps, and two test pilots from each of the aircraft manufacturers were invited to participate. Notably, the joint service pilot roster included Major Tom Lanphier, who was credited with the shoot-down of Japanese Admiral Isoruko Yamamoto eight months before, Major Joseph Myers, who would become an ace and was credited with the first shoot-down of an Me-262 jet fighter later that year, and Lieutenant Ken Walsh, already a Marine Corps Corsair ace with 400 hours in type who was awarded a Medal of Honor by President Franklin Roosevelt the month after the conference.

Boone Guyton introduced the two fighters that Vought brought to the conference: the F4U-1 originally from the Vought production line and the F3A-1 from Brewster, ferried in from Naval Air Station Jacksonville: "Both have water injection, raised cabins and raised tail wheels. . . . The [F3A-1] has the wing fold taken out and also we have a wing tank [F4U-1] hooked up for 60 gallons of water; the other aircraft [F3A-1], a normal production aircraft with 10.3 gallons of water and alcohol. . . . There is a spoiler on the right-hand leading edge of each airplane, mainly there for stalling both wings evenly under acceleration and turns or pull-outs."[6] Guyton apparently did not mention that its primary purpose was mitigating the wing drop on carrier landings. During the conference, in between scheduled evaluation flights, Guyton in the F4U-1 and Lieutenant Walsh in the F3A-1 met in the air for three simulated combat engagements. Guyton admitted that, even with the advantage of more water for war emergency power, he was defeated soundly each time by the combat-experienced Walsh.

Interestingly, no Navy pilots flew the Corsairs during the conference. The Army, Marine, Royal Air Force, and contractor pilots that did were given five categories in which to record their findings: cockpit arrangement, taxiing view, airborne pilot "ease," landing and roll, and general discussion. Comments on cockpit arrangement ranged from "fair" to "poor." One item in particular had to do with placement of carbon dioxide bottles in the cockpit and their respective actuation switches. One bottle was for blowing down the landing gear in the event of a hydraulic failure; the other was for inerting the atmosphere in the fuel tank to prevent explosive ignition should the tank be penetrated by enemy gunfire. Vought relocated the two bottles and provided an additional safety lever to the landing gear release. These fixes would appear in later Corsair models. Taxiing view drew the expected comments about difficulty seeing over the nose, but there were positive notes about raising the seat posture. The Bell Aircraft test pilot provided a few well-considered comments that nicely summarized all of the general input regarding the Corsair: "a very good fighter with excellent performance for its type and very efficient considering the gap between stalling speed and top speed. . . . Needs major cockpit redesign and more labor-saving devices such as automatic cooling shutters, synchronized throttle and propeller control, and automatic manifold pressure regulation."[7]

NAVY INTEREST GAINS TRACTION

Monitoring the Grumman and Vought test flights in the spring of 1944 with keen interest was Commander Paul Ramsey, recently returned from fighter squadron command in the Pacific where he tangled with the Japanese Zeke and was now director of flight test at Patuxent River Naval Air Station, Maryland. Ramsey's take on the outcome of these comparative assessments was captured in a memorandum to the BuAer fighter design desk wherein he ascribed to the Hellcat better stability and low speed control, better service maintenance, and simpler and better cockpit arrangement. Yet, he asserted that the Corsair had the advantage of considerably better speed performance, better high-speed control, and relative quiet and comfort in the cockpit. He concluded that "on balance, the F4U was the better military ship as a day fighter airplane . . . and it is recommended that the F4U type airplane again be employed as a combat carrier type."[8]

That same month, with newer versions of both airplanes rapidly filling out the inventory of both Navy and Marine fighter squadrons, Commander Naval Air Forces Pacific Fleet, Rear Admiral Charles Pownall, promoted a head-to-head fly-off comparison between the F4U-1D and F6F-5 in Hawaii in May 1944. The evaluators were three combat-experienced squadron commanders: Lieutenant Commander Gordon Cady, commanding officer of VF-11, Lieutenant Commander Bernard Strean, commanding officer of VF-1, and Lieutenant Colonel John Smith, former commanding officer of VMF-223 at Guadalcanal. Cady and Smith had flown the F4F Wildcat, while Strean had flown the F6F-3 Hellcat. The three pilots were given a window of time for flight deck availability with a carrier escort operating off San Diego for carrier landing evaluation. All three made several landings and determined that "the F4U-1D was equally as good a carriers airplane as the F6F-5, if not better."[9] They assessed that the F6F-5 was not any more maneuverable than the F4U-1D, confirming the experience of the Grumman test team. Stick forces were lighter in F4U-1D maneuvers. And finally, all agreed the Corsair was a more stable gun platform and a more accurate dive-bomber.[10] This was high praise indeed from fighter squadron skippers whose experience was shaped by aerial combat in Grumman aircraft.

As if everyone in a position to witness the Corsair's improving performance had an opinion to share, Commander Fleet Air Quonset Point, Rear Admiral Calvin T. Durgin, also in May 1944 penned a speed letter to Commander Air Forces Atlantic Fleet, Vice Admiral Pat Bellinger, extolling the Corsair's virtues. Durgin's command was gaining hands-on experience with the F4U-1D in the initial East Coast familiarization training for new Corsair pilots. He reported that the Corsair's

> carrier landing characteristic has been greatly improved by the incorporation of the "bounce eliminator" in the landing gear . . . as a result the average landing compares favorably in smoothness with other carrier types. Due to the large flap area of the Corsair, it decelerates rapidly after cutting the throttle, normally resulting in a shorter run-out of the arresting wire than with the Hellcat. The cruising radius is considerably longer than that of the Hellcat due to the larger gas capacity. The Corsair is more maneuverable, lighter on the controls, and is probably superior to the Hellcat as a fixed gunnery airplane after pilots are well familiarized. And, statistics prepared by [Carrier Aircraft Support Unit 23] at [Naval Air Station] Atlantic City show that the maintenance problem of the Corsair is only slightly greater than that of the Hellcat.[11]

Durgin added his strongest recommendation that additional air groups be equipped with Corsair squadrons as soon as the F4U-4 model could be fielded. Commander Pownall formulated a similar recommendation, although he insisted that F4U-1Ds not replace F6Fs in fleet squadrons but that F4U-4s could as soon as available. Deputy Chief of Naval Operations for Air Rear Admiral Arthur W. Radford, acting for the Chief of Naval Operations, replied to both approving the swap of Corsairs for Hellcats pending the availability of F4U-4s.

JOINT SERVICE FIGHTER CONFERENCE—OCTOBER 1944

Undoubtedly, the broadest and most comprehensive comparison of fighter types—and validation that the Corsair had finally arrived—was conducted at another joint fighter conference, this time hosted by the Navy for one week in October 1944 at the Patuxent River

Naval Air Station. Again, pilots representing the Army, Navy, Marine Corps, Royal Air Force, and Royal Navy, as well as test pilots from the major fighter producers, were invited to put service aircraft through exhaustive test flights and critique. One producer not invited was Mitsubishi, whose A6M5 model 52 recently captured on Saipan was provided on the ramp for evaluation. The purpose, as before in January, was cross-pollination, to apply the wealth of experience in fighter performance across the many represented services, and to tease out from the evaluation debriefs areas for improvement in all types. It is noteworthy that Navy participants included Commander C. T. Booth, who had done the earlier carrier suitability assessment flights at Jacksonville, Commander R. E. Harmer, just returning from command of VF(N)-101 in the Pacific flying F4U-2 night-fighters in combat, and conference chairman Commander Paul Ramsey. From the Army, Major Tom Lanphier made another appearance, as did Corky Meyer, Grumman's chief engineering test pilot who had flown the Corsair in the BuAer-sanctioned tests the prior summer. Vought attendees included chief engineer Russ Clark and, among a roster of test pilots, the earliest Corsair pilots, Lyman Bullard and Boone Guyton.

In the plenary session, Guyton was called on for opening remarks from Vought. He announced that the company brought F4U-1D and F4U-1C airplanes for the evaluation program and added that a prototype of the newest in the Corsair series, the F4U-4X, was also available for examination. Goodyear's representative allowed that they had provided one FG-1 for flight and one F2G-1 with Pratt & Whitney's Wasp Major engine for inspection. In the introductions, a BuAer representative also spoke about a new material for F4U control surfaces that had the Navy's attention—an aluminum alloy bonded with balsa wood material showing increased bending and torsion strength with no increase in weight. The new structural material would be accorded a commercial identity, Metalite, and would be a candidate for F4U-4 ailerons and stabilizers.

Lieutenant J. P. M. Reid, Royal Navy Volunteer Reserve, was one of the three British pilots participating in the October 1944 fighter conference that flew and critiqued the F4U-1D. Here, Reid goes through his preflight cockpit checks. (Tommy Thomason)

F4U-1D as flown by VBF-83 aboard USS *Essex*, spring 1945. (Artwork by Gaëtan Marie, Bravo Bravo Aviation)

F4U-1D vs. A6M5-52b

	F4U-1D			A6M5-52b
As Flown:	12,014 lbs Full Ammo Engine - P&W R2800-8W			6,094 lbs Full Ammo Engine - Nakajima Sakae 21
	Rating*			**Rating****
Power Loading	4.8 lbs/bhp	✓		5.3 lbs/bhp
Wing Loading	38.5 lbs/ft²		✓	26.3 lbs/ft²
Turn Rate	"Don't try to turn with a Zeke"		✓	Superior
Roll Rate	Superior above 250 kts	✓		Approx. equal below 250 kts
Top Speed @ 20k'	416 mph (W.E.P.)	✓		335 mph
Climb Rate to 20k'	3,110 ft/min 700 ft/min greater from 10k' to 20k'	✓		2,812 ft/min Equal up to 10,000'
Visibility	Blown Canopy = improved viz	✓		Birdcage Canopy limits vision
Vulnerability	Armor & Self-sealing tanks	--	--	Armor and self-sealing tanks (added beginning with -52b)

Power Loading = Gross Weight ÷ Brake Horsepower / Higher P.L. = better climb rate and faster acceleration
Wing Loading = Gross Weight ÷ Wing Area / Lower W.L. = good instantaneous turn performance and turn rate
Higher Top Speed = maneuvering advantage for faster closure with target, or faster separation from engagement

* M.H. Tuttle, CDR, USN, "Combat Evaluation of Zeke 52 with F4U-1D"
** René J. Francillon, *Japanese Aircraft of the Pacific War*

Commander M. H. Tuttle, USN, "Combat Evaluation of the Zeke 52 with F4U-1D"; René Francillon, *Japanese Aircraft of the Pacific War*

Mitsubishi (Nakajima) A6M5 52b of 313 Hikotai/221 Kokutai Asanbara, late 1944. (Artwork by Dave Douglas, research by Ryan Toews)

After each evaluation flight, the pilot filled in a comment card that recorded data and opinions, ranging from "good" to "poor" to "liked it very much." A blank area on the card was left for detailed comments. As might be expected, the F6F-5 and F4U-1D were flown most by Army pilots and contractor pilots other than Vought representatives, who all had little previous exposure to the models. Opinions were remarkably consistent with Navy and Marine experience in the field. The Hellcat scored high praise for cockpit layout and comfort, while the Corsair cockpit drew more negative cockpit comments such as "untidy—too many gadgets" and "poor forward visibility." These comments varied little from what had been received in the earlier fighter conference. In more subjective but critical areas like combat qualities, the Hellcat was thought by one pilot to be "maneuverability-limited by longitudinal and lateral stability," but with "sufficient combat qualities for fighting present Japanese planes, though probably not fast enough in near future." In combat qualities, the Corsair, beyond its noted limitations in cockpit layout and visibility, was thought to be "a very fine fighting airplane with great possibilities."[12]

When all the grades and comments for the week were tallied and summed for all fighter types including the Navy F6F-5 and Army Air Forces P-38s, P-47s, and P-51s, the Corsair ranked first in armor protection, first in flight control sensitivity and responsiveness, first in dive performance, first in multi-mission fighter-bomber performance, best as overall fighter below 25,000 feet altitude, and perhaps surprisingly, first in carrier approach handling. Owing much to the soundness of the original design, but equally to the diligence, engineering acumen, and industry of the Vought team—chief engineer Russ Clark, project engineer Paul Baker, test pilot Boone Guyton, and field service rep Jack Hospers—and to the early adopters and advocates—the many Marine Corsair fighter squadrons, and particularly the work of Navy squadron VF-17—the F4U was finally coming into its own, leaving behind the disparaged reputation it had acquired in the first two years of war. Its qualities would be soon measured more broadly against an increasingly desperate and fanatical foe.

Before the aircraft assessments wrapped up, Navy participants added one more set of head-to-head engagements to test the F4U-1D against the captured A6M5 Model 52. "From sea level up to 30,000 feet, the Corsair proved faster by an average of 55 knots (63 mph)." In rate of climb, the Corsair and Zeke were fairly evenly matched up to 10,000 feet, when the Corsair began to pull away. At slower speeds, the Zeke had the advantage in turn rate, but the Corsair could stay with the Zeke through a first half-turn by judicious use of flaps. After that first half-turn, the Zeke gained the advantage as the Corsair's airspeed continued to bleed off. Roll rate was comparable at or slightly below 200 mph. But above 200 mph, air loads on the Zeke required increasingly more stick force to stay with the Corsair's roll rate.[13] If this last assessment between Corsair and Zeke yielded useful tactical information for aerial battles to come, in the main it reaffirmed what had been learned in the demanding battles in the Solomons: Use Corsair's advantage in airspeed and climb rate to drag the Zeke into the vertical when possible—don't persist in a hard level turning fight where the Corsair's edge will evaporate; and when possible, initiate the engagement with slashing attack from higher altitude to hold the Zeke centered in the gunsight until diving through at high speed. the joint fighter conference that conferred so much fresh confidence in the Corsair's bona fides ended on Monday, 23 October 1944. On Wednesday, halfway around the globe, the USS *St. Lo* (CVE-63) became the first major U.S. warship sunk by aircraft attack from a new Japanese weapon, the Kamikaze.

NOTES

1. Clark G. Reynolds, *The Fast Carriers* (Annapolis, MD: Naval Institute Press, 1992), 22.

2. Henry Sakaida, *Imperial Japanese Navy Aces 1937–1945* (Oxford: Osprey Publishing, 1999), 82.

3. Masatake Okumiya and Jiro Horikoshi, *Zero* (New York: E. P. Dutton, 1956), 221–22.

4. Trapnell and Tibbetts, *Harnessing the Sky*, 101.

5. Corky Meyer, "Hellcat versus Corsair—Grumman Test Pilot Flies the Competition," 17 November 2020, https://www.pressreader.com/usa/wwii-fighters/20201117/281603833007728.

6. Guyton, *Whistling Death*, 257.

7. Jack Woolams, in Guyton, *Whistling Death*, 262.

8. Paul H. Ramsey, "Memorandum for the VF Design Desk," NA83-FT-44016, May 1944, National Archives and Records Administration, College Park, MD.

9. Correspondence with Bernard M. Strean, 10 June 1978, in Tillman, *Corsair*, 18.

10. Tillman, *Corsair*.

11. C. T. Durgin, "Proposed Use of F4U Aircraft in Carrier Air Groups," 28 June 1944, http://www.researcheratlarge.com/Aircraft/F4U/F4UCarrierSuitability.html.

12. Francis H. Dean, ed., *Report of Joint Fighter Conference* (Atglen, PA: Schiffer Publishing, 1998), 252–67.

13. Tillman, *Corsair*, 20.

CORSAIRS VS. KAMIKAZES

The F4U-1D was found superior to the latest Japanese model. The edge over the Frank and George is not large but is ample to gain victory by an aggressive attack.

—Commander Raymond E. Hill[1]

Due to excessive distances between mid-Pacific islands, Marine Corsairs were typically transported by escort carriers to populate captured airfields, where they flew base defense and close air support missions if the islands were still contested. (NARA)

The mass suicide raids launched against the fleet made it impossible to intercept every Kamikaze, but the Marines' efforts saved countless lives and the aircraft they flew would earn the nickname the "Sweetheart of Okinawa" for its contribution during Operation Iceberg.

—"Sweetheart of Okinawa: Kadena's Corsair Squadrons"[2]

MARINE CORSAIRS GO TO SEA

The Solomon Islands campaign yielded a strategic win for Allied forces. In February 1944 the Japanese realized the tenuousness of their position and withdrew from Rabaul, leaving only a remnant to garrison what had been a fortified bastion. Their naval and air stronghold had been neutralized, and with that, the threat to the left flank of Admiral Chester Nimitz's central Pacific campaign had been diminished. To avoid the unacceptably high casualties that would result from an amphibious invasion, Rabaul was bypassed. Marine and Navy shore-based Corsairs made a crucial difference. They provided the range, endurance, and performance necessary to meet and beat back the Japanese aerial onslaught, a feat that could not have been achieved with the F4F Wildcats that initially defended Guadalcanal. Corsairs, flown to the limit of their performance by their Navy and Marine aviators, tipped the balance, clearing the way for amphibious forces to hopscotch from Guadalcanal to the Russells, to the New Georgia Islands, to Bougainville, and finally, into the Bismarck Archipelago.

As the central Pacific campaign got underway, however, the months spent taking back the Solomons allowed the Japanese time to fortify defenses on the Gilberts, Marshalls, Marianas, and Palaus. Storming these far-flung island bastions required air support from carrier-borne planes. Other than the limited participation of night-fighting F4U-2s on the carriers, F6F Hellcats now took center stage. Marine fighter squadrons, toughened by more than a year of fighting their Corsairs, were relegated to backwater duty reducing Japanese garrisons on bypassed islands—though Japanese resistance in the form of anti-aircraft barrage was still vigorous and lethal on many of the islands. As central Pacific islands were overrun, Marine Corsairs were ferried in by transport escort carriers (CVEs) to fly as a base defense and to support further gains on the ground. But their offensive air-to-air role was greatly scaled back due to lack of aerial opposition.

Marine commandant General Alexander "Archie" Vandegrift did not want to see the Corsair capability underused or permitted to atrophy. With his deputies, Major General Gerald Thomas, director of Marine Corps plans and policies, and Major General Field Harris, director of Marine Corps aviation, he met with Commander-in-Chief Pacific Admiral Nimitz, Nimitz's deputy, Vice Admiral John Towers, and Rear Admiral Forrest Sherman, Nimitz's deputy chief of staff in August 1944 at Pearl Harbor, to propose a course of action. The agreement, largely the work of Admiral Sherman, provided that Marine Corsair squadrons would serve on escort carriers. In implementation, Marine air groups each composed of an 18-plane Corsair fighter squadron and 12-plane bombing squadron of TBM Avengers would embark in 4 CVEs, with another 2 CVEs hosting Navy air groups for overhead protection of the small task group of 6 CVEs.

A mix of F4U-1Ds and FG-1Ds made up the fighter squadrons in the first four Marine air groups to be commissioned, all with the carrier landing issues corrected and with D modifications that gave them greater ground attack capability. Carrier landing practice commenced immediately off San Diego. In February 1944 carrier training had been completed, and all four Marine Corsair squadrons in the first Marine air support group were assigned their carriers, beginning with VMF-511 (with eight F4U-1Ds or FG-1Ds) to USS *Block Island*. The other three Corsair squadrons were assigned to their carriers at one-month intervals thereafter: VMF-512 (with 17 F4U-1Ds or FG-1Ds) to USS *Gilbert Islands*, VMF-513 (with 16 F4U-1Ds or FG-1Ds) to USS *Vella Gulf*, and VMF-351 (with 15 FG-1Ds) to USS *Cape Gloucester*.[3] Ultimately, nine squadrons deployed aboard escort carriers in 1945, four of which saw combat in the Philippines and Okinawa.[4]

A new peril, kamikaze attacks, imposed an unforeseen and distressing reality on campaign planning at all levels of command. Vice Admiral Marc Mitscher, commander of Task Force 58, knew the situation had to be addressed immediately before U.S. naval forces encountered greater numbers of kamikazes in the spring campaigns. Responding to urgent requests from his carrier task group commanders for more fighters, Mitscher saw Chief of Naval Operations Admiral King in Washington to propose that Marine fighter squadrons with their Corsairs be pressed into service on the big deck carriers as a stopgap measure to provide more fighter capacity to counter the kamikaze. King endorsed the idea, and commander Air Forces Pacific, Vice Admiral George D. Murray, decreed that ten Marine fighter squadrons would augment Navy fighter squadrons aboard big-deck *Essex*-class ships.[5] Navy fighter strength in the carrier air group would be increased by the addition of two 18-aircraft Marine fighter squadrons composed of F4U-1D Corsairs. For the moment, the impetus behind Marine carrier air groups bound for ground support duty on escort carriers was eclipsed by Marine fighter squadrons joining Navy air groups to repel the new menace. Over the next few months, five *Essex* carriers would host the ten Marine Corsair squadrons.

Once aboard CVEs for regular operations from the carrier, there was usually a break-in period for Marine pilots. VMF-351 had qualified for carrier landings on USS *Ranger* (CV-4) in late 1944, then on USS *Commencement Bay* (CVE-105) in February 1945, and finally on USS *Cape Gloucester* (CVE-109) in April to support operations off Okinawa. This VMF-351 Corsair has suffered significant damage after hitting the barricade on *Cape Gloucester*. (Matthew Acred at https://www.asisbiz.com/mla.html)

CORSAIRS STRIKE AT THE EMPIRE

First to be assigned big-deck carrier duty were VMF-124 and VMF-213 in December 1944 on board USS *Essex* (CV-9). They were soon in combat, flying from the *Essex* as part of Task Force 38. War diary entries[6] recorded on two days in mid-February provide a glimpse of the action as it moved from strikes on the fringe of the Japanese home island of Kyushu to the Japanese home islands toward Iwo Jima:

> On February 17, 1945, Captain W. J. Thomas led a flight of 7 F4Us escorting 13 TBMs into, over and back from Nakajima Tama Aircraft Engine Plant on the northwestern edge of Tokyo. A total of twenty-four Tony's (Kawasaki Ki-61), Oscars (Nakajima Ki-43) and Tojo's (Nakajima Ki-44) annoyed the formation throughout their approach and final bombing run. First to attack were four Zeke's, reddish brown with big red meatballs. . . . They slow-rolled as they went by. By the end of the mission, Marine Corsairs scored seven confirmed shoot downs.
>
> Two days later on the 19th, Lt Col Millington led a flight of twenty-four F4Us and twenty-four F6Fs to support the initial landings on Iwo Jima by attacking the flanks and high ground along the landing beaches with napalm and rockets, strafing the beaches just ahead of the landings. The flight was split into two elements for the flank attacks, with twelve F4Us carrying napalm and rockets on each flank. The attacks were delivered from a double-column approach with divisions breaking to port and starboard as assigned, dropping napalm on the first run, pulling out to the east, and repeating attacks with rockets and strafing.

If there was a teething problem bringing Marine Corsairs aboard carriers, it was shown to be more the result of foul weather than of the aircraft's adaptability to carrier decks as in the past. Nor were these two Marine Corsair squadrons alone in the task force. In addition to VMF-124 and -213 on *Essex*, other carriers now hosted complements of F4Us. Two squadrons of Corsairs, VMF-112 and -123, had joined Air Group 82 on *Bennington*, VMF-214 and -452 were now with Air Group 5 on *Franklin*, and -221 and -451 joined Air Group 84 on *Bunker Hill*. As Task Force 58—renumbered from Task Force 38 to reflect a rotating change in commanders and staff—prepared for operations off Okinawa, several Marine squadrons were offloaded for refit and rest and were replaced by a growing number of Navy Corsairs units. VMF-124 and -213 in *Essex* were rotated off making room for Navy Bombing Fighting Squadron 83, while VMF-216 and -217 were rotated off *Wasp* to be replaced by Navy squadron VBF-86, the "Vapor Trails." Veteran Corsair pilots from Tom Blackburn's reformed VF-17 "Jolly Rogers" seeded *Bunker Hill*'s VF-84 "Wolf Gang" with John Ellsworth, Chico Freeman, Jimmy Smith, and ace Roger Hedrick as commanding officer. Smith and Freeman would become aces in the months

An F4U-1D of VBF-83 comes aboard USS *Essex* (CV-9) in spring 1945, paired with VF-83's F6F-5 Hellcats in the *Essex* air group. The Corsair squadron beat the Hellcat squadron to the scoreboard by downing 18 Japanese airplanes on 18 March. (NARA)

The "Wolf Gang" of VF-84 added 27 Corsairs to the 36 Marine Corsairs in Air Group 84 aboard USS *Bunker Hill* (CV-17). Here, a VF-84 F4U-1D steadies up in the groove with his hook down for landing on *Bunker Hill*. VF-84 Corsairs would take part in the attacks on Japanese battleship *Yamato* on 7 April. (NARA)

ahead, flying F4U-1Ds. Within just a few months, increasing numbers of F4U-1Cs were introduced into the squadron. More VF-17 Corsair veterans seeded VF-10's "Grim Reapers" on *Intrepid*, including Timmy Gile, William Landreth, Dave Cunningham, Wally Schub, and Paul Cordray, three of whom were already Corsair aces from their time flying with VF-17 in the Solomons. VBF-6 "Whistling Death" came aboard *Hancock* with F4U-1Ds, *Franklin* hosted VF-5 "Screaming Eagles" with 18 F4U-1Ds, and *Shangri-La* joined Task Group (TG) 58.4 in late April with VF-85 "Sky Pirates" operating a mix of F4U-1Ds and F4U-1Cs.

Task Force 58's eight Marine Corsair squadrons flew ground support missions and combat air patrol (CAP) over the carriers for only four days of the campaign for Iwo Jima before departing on D+3, leaving support to the three Marine divisions for the rest of the five-week land battle to Navy escort carrier squadrons and, eventually, Army P-51 Mustangs.[7] In contrast, Marines at Okinawa would persist by moving ashore for the duration of the campaign and, in the process, making real their long-held aspiration for a tightly coordinated air-ground team. At Okinawa, however, stopping the onslaught of suicide planes targeting the fleet took priority over direct close air support of the advancing Marine infantry.[8]

Task Force 58 sortied from the Ulithi anchorage on 14 March to carry out Operation Iceberg, the invasion and capture of Okinawa. First, outlying airfields that could serve to interrupt the operation had to be reduced. In the weeks that followed, Corsairs from TGs 58.1 (*Wasp* and *Bennington*) and 58.3 (*Essex*, *Bunker Hill*, and *Hancock*) concentrated on Japanese warships at the Kure shipyard, while TG 58.4 (*Intrepid*) struck facilities at Kobe, and 58.2 (*Franklin*) hit naval air installations at Kure. Punctuating the series of strikes on in-port vessels and naval facilities, all of the task force's Corsair squadrons joined the Hellcat squadrons for fighter sweeps over airfields on Kyushu to reduce Japanese capacity to launch conventional bombing and kamikaze attacks against the amphibious ships pulled up to the shoreline for the invasion.

"OKINAWA GUNTO WILL BE DESPERATELY RESISTED"[9]

Kamikazes and bombers still got through. Okinawa was well within range—particularly for one-way suicide flights—from Japanese airfields on the more northerly Ryukyu Islands, from Kyushu, and from Formosa. The U.S. Navy's Task Force 58, operating in the vicinity of Okinawa, was under constant threat of air attack. By the time Task Force 58 took station off Okinawa on 23 March to begin flying CAPs over the invasion fleet, *Wasp* and *Franklin* had retired, lost to bomb damage, thereby reducing the number of available Corsairs by more than 80 aircraft. That day also saw the positioning of an early-warning screen of radar picket stations (RPs) around Okinawa, each station anchored by specially equipped destroyer-type ships acting as the fighter director for its sector, accompanied by two large landing craft ships outfitted as gunboats to add firepower. Eventually, 20 RPs would be established, but fewer were occupied on a full-time basis so as to vex arriving Japanese attackers. On 1 April—L-day for the initial landings on Okinawa—and throughout the month, eight RPs were up and running. In the first week of invasion, the primary function of Task Force 58 fighter aircraft—its Corsairs and Hellcats—was to provide the

CAP over the RPs. When the situation was quiet, a division (four aircraft) of Corsairs or Hellcats would normally orbit the RP. When alerted to the approach of enemy formations, the CAP might surge to as many as four divisions stacked at varying altitudes over the RP. Depending on demand, most carriers in the task force supplied fighters for CAPs. Corsair squadrons flying CAPs singled out for mention in action reports included VF-10 from *Intrepid*, VMF-112 and -123 from *Bennington*, and VF-84, VMF-221, and VMF-451 from *Bunker Hill*.

During the initial five days of landings, opposition was not as forceful as expected, with only random, seemingly unorganized yet persistent attacks by Japanese aircraft. The strikes and fighter sweeps by the task force in the weeks before the landings seemed to have suppressed the expected surge in aerial attacks from the Japanese. And, too, at Okinawa, the Japanese emphasis changed from taking a toll on amphibious infantry to exacting unacceptable attrition on the offshore fleet, and to accomplish that by suicide attack.

It started with a fury on 6 April. On that day began the first of ten *kikusui* (floating chrysanthemum), or mass suicide, attacks that continued over a six-week span targeting the U.S. amphibious fleet and capital warships. On 6 April alone, 355 Japanese suicide planes, accompanied by 344 aircraft escorts or bombers, came at the task force in several waves over the daylight hours.[10] TG 58.1, deployed farthest north toward Kyushu with the two Marine Corsair squadrons in *Bennington*, took the brunt of the onslaught. TG 58.3, with more than 100 Corsairs embarked in three carriers, remained in close proximity. TG 58.4 did not arrive with its 66 F4U-1Ds embarked in *Intrepid* from out-of-area refueling until the next day, and 58.2 remained off the line for refueling.

RPs 1, 2, and 3, the first that the Japanese would encounter on their way toward the larger concentration of U.S. warships, were getting saturated but continued vectoring the combat air patrol overhead. At noon, a division of four Corsairs of VMF-112 from *Bennington* answered a vector call from USS *Cassin Young* on RP 2. The flight was led by squadron skipper Major Herman Hansen, and each of his two sections took divergent headings for separation. The second section sighted the first Japanese at lower altitude as they passed through a cumulus patch, immediately going into a high-speed dive to give chase. The Japanese dived to escape but had great difficulty maneuvering and simply flew into the water, exploding on impact. Minutes later, Major Hansen sighted his own Zeke just as the Japanese pilot attempted a split-S maneuver to escape. Hansen pushed over to catch him at the start of his dive, but the negative G force jammed the ammunition linkage, causing a temporary stoppage of his guns. Briefly distracted, he didn't observe the Zeke pulling hard back into his flight path: "It looked like a certain collision. I pulled back on the stick but barely cleared the tail and fuselage with my prop. I figure I wasn't more than 12 inches above him. I could see the rivets in his airplane. I saw the pilot clearly. Lashed beneath the plane was a big bomb. It was suspended by a makeshift arrangement of wires or ropes. The ropes flapped in the wind."[11] As the two aircraft passed, opening the distance between them, Hansen's wingman, 2nd Lieutenant George J. Murray, opened fire in a high-angle deflection shot. As Murray drew within feet, the Zeke erupted in a billowing plume of flame, smoke, and aircraft parts.

TG-58.1 and TG-58.3 fighters—Corsairs and Hellcats—shot down no fewer than 233 of the attacking Japanese aircraft. Fighters from the CVEs disposed of another 55, and the ships' anti-aircraft fire took down 39 more. Marine Corsairs from *Bunker Hill* knocked down 12, while *Bennington*'s Corsairs on CAP shot down another 5.[12]

KIKUSUI FROM SEA AND THE AIR

7 April began with a sighting report at 8:32 a.m. by search planes from TG 58.1, warning of a Japanese surface fleet moving south in the direction of Okinawa, centered on *Yamato*. The monster battleship and her escorts were playing their part in the day's suicide blitz, intending to wreak havoc and destruction among the amphibious force ships. At ten o'clock, TGs 58.1 and 58.3 launched a 280-plane strike that included 15 VF-84 Corsairs from *Bunker Hill*, armed with a single 500-pound bomb and high-velocity aircraft rockets, and a lone VMF-112 Corsair from *Bennington* similarly armed. *Hancock*'s strike group launched late and would not find *Yamato*, reducing the strike formation to 227 fighters, bombers, and torpedo bombers. Most of *Bennington*'s ready Corsairs were already committed to CAP stations over the radar pickets that day. The only available Marine Corsair pilot on *Bennington*'s flight deck was 2nd Lieutenant Ken Huntington, a young Kansas State engineering graduate who lacked extensive combat experience but who

understood the urgency of the situation. He sat with his Navy Helldiver compatriots in Bombing 82's ready room for the prestrike briefing as an ordnance crew uploaded his Corsair on the flight deck above.

After launch, as the strike formed up and took an intercept heading, Huntington joined on Air Group 82's SB2Cs and TBMs, intending to make his bombing run in turn with the other bombers. Arriving over the Japanese surface group, nearly simultaneously with the other carrier air groups from TG 58.3, U.S. planes circled within sight of the Japanese, just out of range, to establish the order and line of attack. At 12:37 p.m., *Bennington*'s air group started down on its attack runs, with fighters leading the bombers in by strafing and firing rockets to clear the decks of anti-aircraft gun crews. Helldivers from *Bennington* and *Hornet* came in on *Yamato*'s port side and dropped several bombs close aboard. None struck home until Huntington's lone Corsair came in behind the first wave of SB2Cs and scored a hit with a 1,000-pound armor-piercing bomb. Detonating just aft of the forward mounts, it knocked out one of *Yamato*'s two air search radars, the aft secondary gun director, and several 25-mm gun mounts, and started a fire that killed all but one crewman in the aft secondary gun turret. Minutes later, 14 more Corsairs from *Bunker Hill* made their strafing and rocket attacks, followed in their runs by *Hornet* TBMs on torpedo runs. One torpedo hit home. Huntington would be presented the Navy Cross for the action.

A VMF-112 Corsair begins a run down the flight deck. One of two Marine Corsair squadrons in the *Bennington* air group, VMF-112 joined in strikes around Tokyo in February 1945, downing 5 aircraft; then, sweeps over Kyushu on 18 March downed another 9, and finally on combat air patrol over Okinawa, another 18 Japanese aircraft that were most likely flown by suicide pilots. (NARA)

More Corsairs joined Hellcats and Avengers in working over the escort destroyers, sinking or disabling four and seriously damaging a fifth. The first wave pulled off, ordnance mostly expended, when the second wave of U.S. attackers from *Essex* and CVE *Bataan* arrived 15 minutes later. An *Essex* Corsair scored a direct hit with a 1,000-pound general purpose bomb on *Yamato*'s port bow. At 1:30 p.m., 110 aircraft from TG 58.4's *Yorktown*, *Intrepid*, and CVE *Langley* arrived. *Intrepid* sent 16 Corsairs—4 F4U-1Ds from VF-10's Grim Reapers, and another 12 Corsairs from VBF-10—into the fray as escorts for Air Group Ten's Helldivers. Lieutenant G. D. Weems leading the VF-10 Corsair division came in with the bombers, making his attack on one of the destroyers screening *Yamato*

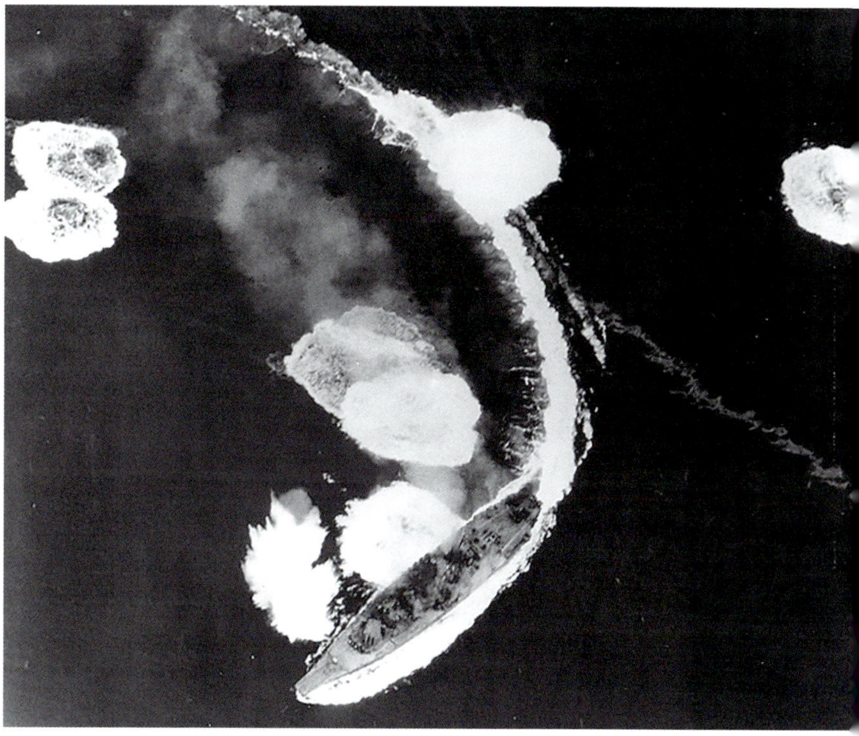

Task Force 58 aircraft bracket the massive Japanese battleship *Yamato* on 7 April, among them Corsairs from VF-84, VF-10, VBF-10, VBF-83, and VMF-112. (Alamy)

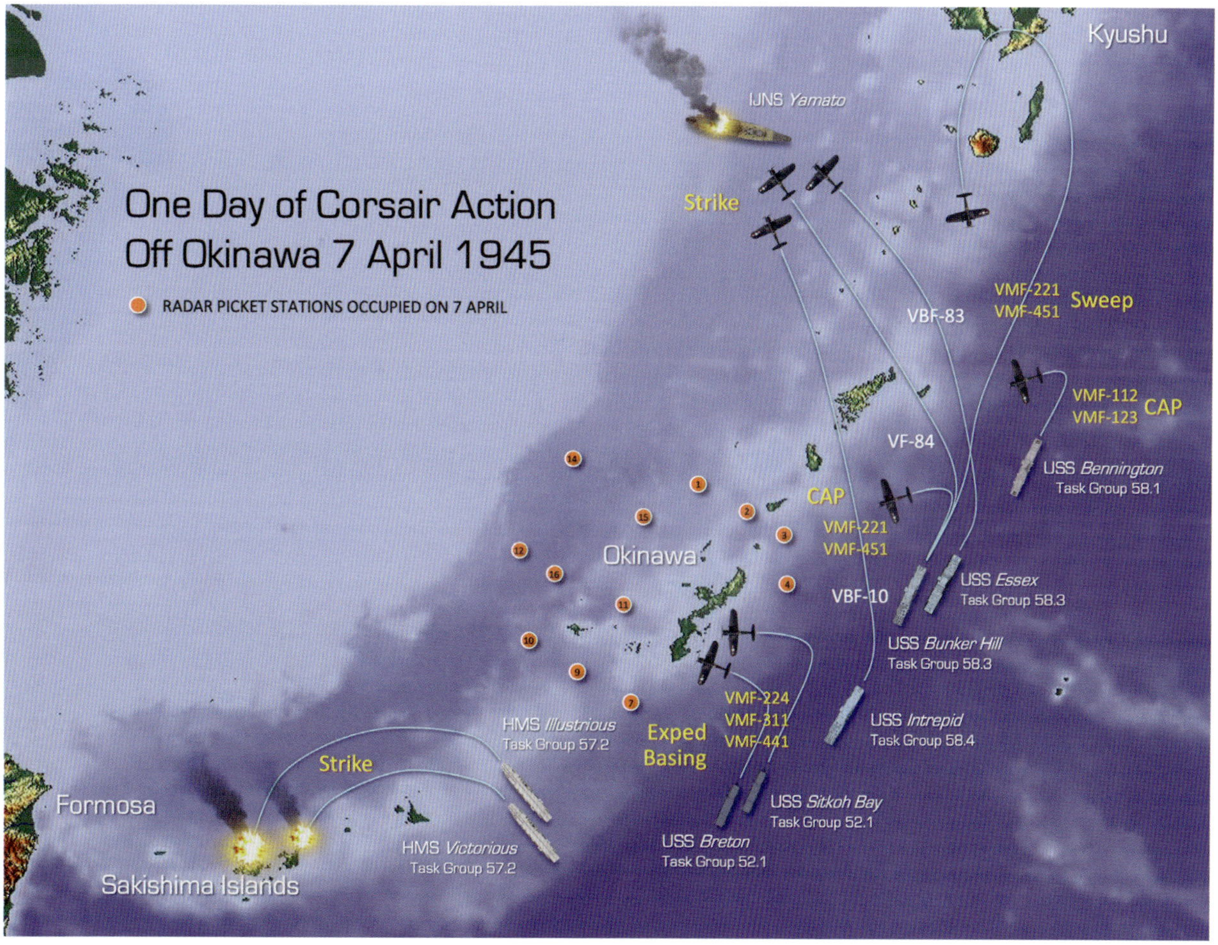

One day of action in and around Okinawa involved close to 200 Navy, Marine, and Fleet Air Arm Corsairs in defensive combat air patrols over the task force, fighter sweeps over Kyushu, and maritime strikes on the Japanese navy surface group centered on battleship *Yamato*. (Artwork by Aldo Spadoni)

while the bombers flew on to continue the attacks on the battleship. Weems' bomb exploded only two yards behind the stern of the *Terutsuki*-class escort that had been making about 25 knots. The ship went into a 180-degree turn and stopped dead in the water. Seeing opportunity, a VT-10 Avenger made the most of this setup and launched a torpedo that hit home, sinking the destroyer.[13]

Navy Lieutenant (junior grade) Hal Jackson, a veteran of earlier days of F4U-1A flying in the Solomons with the Jolly Rogers and now with VBF-10 in *Intrepid*, flying the F4U-1C, recalled;

> When we pulled off the carrier that day, none of us figured we'd be in for much excitement. But the *Yamato* appeared as clouds dissipated. I led my division down to the deck level in a screaming dive at 400 mph, and each of us released our 1,000-pound bombs as we cleared the ship's conning tower by no more than 1,000 feet. Luck was with me. I was one of the last of about 380 planes to go over, and about 10 minutes after I dropped my bomb, I saw the *Yamato* explode in a million pieces. It was the first battleship I had ever seen go down, and it was a sight I'll never forget.[14]

The many bomb and torpedo hits on *Yamato* finally took a toll, such that by a few minutes after two o'clock, she was rolling over and her crew was abandoning the battleship. At 2:30 p.m., the colossal warship—its very name and loss a metaphor for the demise of the Japanese Empire—was slipping beneath the surface as her forward magazine exploded, issuing a boiling black smoke plume that could be seen for tens of miles.

As *Yamato* met her end, VF-84 from *Bunker Hill* launched another flock of Corsairs to assume CAP over the pickets. Lieutenant Commander Tex Hill, squadron commander, led a flight of four Corsairs to an orbit about 15 miles behind RP 4. The flight came upon Japanese attackers headed for the task force and quickly dispatched one D4Y Judy dive-bomber and two P1Y Frances bombers.

A Marine pilot with VMF-224 "Fighting Wildcats" prepares to be catapulted from USS *Sitkoh Bay* (CVE-86) for shore-basing at Yontan airfield on Okinawa. (Matthew Acred at https://www.asisbiz.com/mla.html)

By 9 April, Marine Air Group 33 was operating from the newly captured Kadena airfield. Here, Corsairs of MAG-33's VMF-323 range over Okinawa from their base at Kadena. (Matthew Acred at https://www.asisbiz.com/mla.html)

DEADLY THREAT OF AERIAL KAMIKAZES PERSISTS

At that very moment that *Yamato* slipped under, Corsairs of Marine Air Group (MAG) 31 were being catapulted from CVEs *Sitkoh Bay* and *Breton*, destined for shore basing at Yontan airfield secured just the night before by Marine infantry. MAG-31's VMF-441 operated F4U-1Ds, while VMF-224 and VMF-311 flew into Yontan with F4U-1Cs. Two days later, following the ground forces' capture of Kadena airfield, MAG-33 arrived with F4U-1D Corsair squadrons VMF-312, -322, and -323. The threat of aerial kamikaze attack persisted well past May, and both Marine air groups were dual-tasked with supporting the ground advance but as a first priority responding to CAP vectoring to protect the fleet offshore. As real estate was taken on Okinawa, more squadrons alighted on those captured and repaired airfields.

The Navy flew F4U-1Cs with VF-84 from *Bunker Hill* beginning in early April 1945 and VF-85 from *Shangri-La*, arriving in late April near Okinawa. Other Marine squadrons equipped with F4U-1Cs would arrive as the campaign unfolded and more airstrips were captured. VMF-314 alighted on Ie Shima once its airstrip was prepared in May. The Navy and Marine F4U-1C squadrons would be fully occupied in strikes on the Japanese home islands, reverting to

Marine Captain Floyd Kirkpatrick of VMF-441 based at Yontan airfield prepares to man his F4U-1D, which he has nicknamed "Palpitatin' Pauli." On 16 April Kirkpatrick intercepted 25 Japanese aircraft targeting one of the radar picket ships as a member of a 12-plane Corsair combat air patrol. Kirkpatrick shot down three bombers on that day, dispersing the rest. (World War Photos at https://www.worldwarphotos.info)

An F4U-1D of VBF-10 from USS *Intrepid* (CV-11) over the amphibious fleet on 1 April 1945, the day of the invasion of Okinawa. (Matthew Acred at https://www.asisbiz.com)

kamikaze screening as scheduled. As to the effectiveness of their F4U-1Cs compared to the lighter rounds carried in F4U-1Ds, Marines flying with VMF-314 reported: "All the pilots were very enthusiastic about the performance of the 20-mm gun. . . . There is no question about hits, because every hit on any part of a plane appears like a gun flash upon impact."[15]

Yamato's end meant the threat of surface action was all but eliminated. The carriers returned their full attention to calls for air support from the ground forces when possible but kept fighters on station over the RPs. At 2:36 p.m. on 7 April, USS *Gregory* (DD-802) en route to RP 3 vectored 8 F4U-1Ds of VF-84 to intercept an incoming flight of 12 P1Y Frances bombers coming down from Kyushu. VF-84 skipper Lieutenant Commander Raymond Hill led the flight in downing two of the intruders while the others scattered. This pattern repeated continuously from the first *kikusui* assault through June as kamikaze and conventional bombing attacks concentrated their challenge to the task force over ten major *kikusui* assaults.

12 April brought the second massed wave of attacks, with 185 kamikazes and 195 bombers and escorts thrown at Task Force 58. Lieutenant (junior grade) Phil Kirkwood, a Duke University graduate just three days shy of his 24th birthday and already an ace with VF-10, was leading a combat air patrol over the pickets when, in airspace dense with approaching Japanese aircraft, he sighted ahead a bogey at 10 miles, several thousand feet below. He took his wingman, Ensign Norwald "Dick" Quiel, into a descending run on the bogey. Kirkwood fired a long burst, scoring hits, but his speed took him past what they could now see was a G4M Betty bomber. Quiel had enough separation from Kirkwood that with a tap on the rudder, he brought his guns to bear for a deflection shot as he too passed by. His burst stitched the bomber's engine nacelle, producing enough fuel-fed fire to spell the bomber's end in a spiraling, flaming descent. By day's end, *Intrepid*'s Corsairs "had gunned down thirteen Vals, one Judy, one Nate, one Jill, and six Zeroes," plus Kirkwood's and Quiel's combined 4, for a total of 26 confirmed kills. Every pilot on the flight schedule that day scored at least one aerial victory.[16]

Four days later, a third *kikusui* wave sent 165 kamikazes against the task force. Three Corsair divisions from *Intrepid* were orbiting near RP 3, stacked at different altitudes. Kirkwood was in the orbit at his prebriefed altitude leading one of the VF-10 divisions, with Dick Quiel again flying as number two on his wing. Rounding out the division, Ensign Horace "Tuck" Heath led the second section with "nugget" Albert Lerch, a 20-year-old ensign from Pennsylvania, flying on his wing as number four in the division. Lerch had been with the squadron only two months, but this day would be his first to feel the surge of adrenaline from firing his .50-caliber guns in aerial combat. Heath's radio was breaking up, which meant that section lead passed to Lerch and placed him as the "shooter" in the two-plane section formation.

Kirkwood and Quiel hung back as Lerch and Heath pressed forward, scanning for a reported inbound flight of Japanese suiciders. Fortune fell in their lap as Quiel, flying a squadron FG-1D that day at a higher perch than Kirkwood, ran into a spread of six Ki-27 Nates. He took down four, a fifth flew into sea, and the sixth eluded him by completing his suicide run on the picket destroyer below. Kirkwood flung himself and his Corsair at another formation of 20 Japanese. In rapid succession, he downed six, a mix of Nates and Vals.[17]

Ensign Lerch, with Heath in tow, sighted 30 more Nates arrayed in characteristic 3-plane wedges. Lerch recalled later for an armed forces radio broadcast: "The two of us just piled into them until they started disappearing and we ran out of ammunition, or we might have kept shooting and gotten more. It was pretty exciting when one or two of them tried to ram me. We believe they were all kamikazes because they were loaded down with bombs and didn't try to jettison them."[18]

Turning into the formation, Lerch didn't see any defensive maneuvering on the part of the Japanese, and it became a very simple exercise to maneuver into position behind each formation wedge, line up the shot, and take the one- to two-second burst of fire to finish off four, with another credited to Heath. They then formed up again as a two-plane section to give chase to three of the Japanese planes that were heading south over Okinawa. The Corsair section quickly dispatched the three-plane Japanese column. Lerch's total for the

A lineup of VF-10 pilots from *Intrepid*. The pilot on the far right is believed to be Lieutenant (junior grade) Phil Kirkwood, who led a division of Corsairs against an overwhelming force of Japanese aircraft on 16 April, earning the Navy Cross. To his left is Lieutenant Dick Quiel, his wingman, who shared with Kirkwood in downing ten Japanese aircraft that day, earning ace status. (Courtesy of George H. Spooner)

Flying as lead of the second section in Phil Kirkwood's VF-10 division on 16 April, Ensign Al Lerch would shoot down seven Japanese airplanes in a single mission, a record matched by only four other Americans in history. (Courtesy of the family of Alfred Lerch)

four-hour flight was seven Japanese aircraft shot down, making him an ace-in-a-day. For Kirkwood's division as a whole, 4 Corsairs took down 20 Japanese airplanes, helping to ease the pressure on the radar pickets below.

This was Lerch's first tangle with Japanese aircraft where he exchanged fire, and it would be his last. That afternoon, a kamikaze leaked through the outer screen to smash into *Intrepid*. The carrier could still recover her own aircraft, but the extent of the damage forced her to depart for Ulithi the next day. From there she sailed on to Pearl Harbor and then to San Francisco for extensive repairs. Once on the West Coast, VF-10 exchanged its F4U-1Ds for newer F4U-4s, the penultimate combat version of the Corsair, to enter the last days of World War II.[19]

NOTES

1. Commander Raymond E. Hill, "CAG 84 Action Reports," 27 May 1945, Record Group 38, National Archives and Records Administration, College Park, MD.

The Grim Reapers

From their commissioning as Fighter Squadron 10 in June 1942, the "Grim Reapers" stood in exceptional company as one of the storied fighter squadrons of World War II in the Pacific. Uniquely, VF-10 was the only squadron to see combat in World War II while operating the Wildcat, the Hellcat, and finally, the Corsair.

Renowned combat leader Lieutenant Commander James Flatley, already a seasoned veteran of the Battle of the Coral Sea, stood up VF-10 and took the squadron into its first combat in the fall of 1942 flying F4F-4s. Reformed in 1943, the "second tour" squadron, with new pilots and a new commanding officer, Lieutenant Commander William R. "Killer" Kane, entered combat with the F6F-3 Hellcat.

Finally, the "third tour" Grim Reaper squadron formed under Lieutenant Commander Wilmer Rawie, another veteran of those early dogfights flying from USS *Enterprise*. To a small nucleus of veteran pilots, Rawie added 67 nugget aviators and 36 enlisted members and began the transition to an initial allotment of 30 F4U-1As.

As new Corsairs were received, the inventory on hand rose to 51 airplanes, which necessitated a split into two squadrons. Rawie assumed command of the newly created VBF-10, and Lieutenant Commander Walter E. Clarke was named commanding officer of VF-10. The squadrons exchanged their F4U-1s for F4U-1Ds, added four F6F-5N night-fighters and embarked in USS *Intrepid*, sailing west on 20 February 1945. *Intrepid*'s air group was one of the rare units with a fighter and bomber-fighter squadron that both flew the F4U-1D.

In action with Task Force 38, then Task Force 58 in and around the Japanese home islands and Okinawa, VBF-10 racked up 10 kills, while VF-10 scored another 87 victories in March and April 1945. Lieutenant Philip R. Kirkwood was the squadron's high scorer in his F4U-1D, with 12 confirmed kills. Damage to *Intrepid* on 16 April forced her retirement from the action and the end of active combat for her two Corsair squadrons.

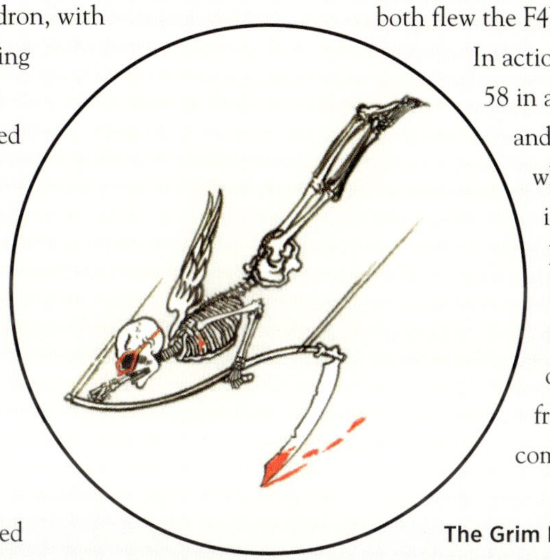

The Grim Reapers squadron insignia. (NHHC)

2. "Sweetheart of Okinawa: Kadena's Corsair Squadrons," 18th Wing History Office, Kadena Air Base News, 10 April 2013, https://www.kadena.af.mil/News/Article/417286/the-sweetheart-of-okinawa-kadenas-corsair-squadrons/.

3. Tillman, *U.S. Marine Corps Fighter Squadrons of World War II*, 252.

4. Sherrod, *History of Marine Corps Aviation*, 450–77.

5. Tillman, *U.S. Marine Corps Fighter Squadrons of World War II*, 117.

6. William A. Millington, "VMF-124 Combat Report," https://airgroup4.com/marines.htm.VMF-124.

7. John Pomeroy Condon, *Corsairs and Flattops* (Annapolis, MD: Naval Institute Press, 1998), 36–39.

8. Vernon Megee, "Evolution of Marine Aviation," oral history transcript (Washington, DC: Historical Division, U.S. Marine Corps, 1973), 2–24.

9. "Battle of Okinawa," Intelligence Digest, Amphibious Forces, Pacific Fleet, April 1945, https://www.nationalww2museum.org/war/topics/battle-of-okinawa.

10. Robin Rielly, *Kamikaze, Corsairs, and Picket Ships* (Havertown, PA: Casemate Press, 2008), 110.

11. VMF (CV)-211 War Diary, 1–30 April 1945, in Rielly, *Kamikaze, Corsairs, and Picket Ships*, 111.

12. Sherrod, *History of Marine Corps Aviation*, 364.

13. W. E. Clark, "VF-10 War History," Record Group 38, National Archives and Records Administration, College Park, MD, https://catalog.archives.gov/id/77659151?objectPage=19.

14. Annetta Ramsay, "Landmarks and Legacies: Hal Jackson Helped Sink Yamato," *Denton* (TX) *Record-Chronicle*, 15 March 2020, https://dentonrc.com/news/landmarks-legacies-hal-jackson-helped-sink-yamato-the-largest-battleship-ever/article_9de56055-6853-57d0-b675-84491b93de57.html.

15. VMF-314 Aircraft Action Report, 3 June 1945, in Rielly, *Kamikaze, Corsairs, and Picket Ships*, 70.

16. Robert Gandt, *The Twilight Warriors* (New York: Crown Publishing, 2010), 242.

17. Gandt, *The Twilight Warriors*, 261.

18. Alfred Lerch, "Voices from the Fleet," recorded interview, ca. 1945, Intrepid Sea, Air, and Space Museum.

19. Clark, "VF-10 War History," 18.

FAA COMES ABOARD

Besides their premium performance, Corsairs had other qualities that helped make them outstanding naval fighters. Unlike some contemporary British aircraft, they featured power-folding wings . . . and thus enabled flight operations to be conducted more expeditiously.

—Michael Whitby, "Navy Blue Fighter Pilot"[1]

A Fleet Air Arm pilot climbs into his Corsair at RAF Wittering, Northamptonshire, in October 1943. (Imperial War Museum, London)

> Our valiant Allies. United we fought. . . .
>
> —Admiral Chester W. Nimitz[2]

When U.S. Navy and Marine Corsairs were given the go-ahead for big-deck carrier operations in the late spring of 1944, Corsairs were already flying in combat from carrier decks but with Britain's Fleet Air Arm (FAA). And these missions were not in the Pacific but in the Atlantic against the Nazi foe. The FAA Corsair debut was in Operation Tungsten on 3 April 1944. In an attempt to knock out the German battleship *Tirpitz* sequestered in a Norwegian fjord, 11 Corsairs were launched from HMS *Victorious* and HMS *Furious* as top cover for Fairy Barracuda bombers in a first wave. Hellcats and Martlets accompanied the formation and came down low to suppress flak guns on the deck with strafing passes. *Tirpitz* shuddered under the impact of multiple bomb hits from the first wave of Barracudas but was not put out of commission. A second wave launched with ten Corsairs from *Victorious* again flying top cover for more Barracudas. The bombers scored multiple direct hits, but none of the bombs penetrated *Tirpitz*'s armor. Three Barracudas and a Hellcat were lost. It seemed that the Luftwaffe was stretched too thin and lacked the capacity to take on the Corsairs for these strikes. *Tirpitz* suffered enough superficial damage that she was taken out of service for three months.

Three months after Tungsten, Operation Mascot launched another 18 Corsairs against *Tirpitz* from the flight deck of HMS *Formidable*. Another attempt at taking out *Tirpitz* followed in August with Operation Goodwood, including 30 Corsairs launched from

Six Fleet Air Arm pilots undergoing conversion training at Lewiston, Maine, fly their Corsairs in formation over the New England countryside. (Imperial War Museum, London)

Formidable for fighter escort duty and dive-bombing if needed. Operation Goodwood played out in several phases, with the final strike on *Tirpitz* coming in late August. Lieutenant Commander Tony Garland, piloting a Corsair II in that attack, recalled;

> The view over the mountains and fjords on this brilliant morning was breathtaking and I could see a whole party of Avengers and the escorting Corsairs of 1841 and 1842 Squadrons. As we approached *Tirpitz*, the white puff of [anti-aircraft] shells started to burst around us and I lost my No. 2, Sub Lieutenant French. The smoke screen was already across the fjord, but leaving a huge outline of the *Tirpitz* just visible through it. I turned and, as I dived, saw one bomb explode close the to the outline of the battleship. I released my bomb and pulled away hard, partially blacking out. There was a lot of flak blazing away in all directions. I turned and fired into one of the gunnery positions, then broke away at low level along the fjord. Cruising along just above the water, I was admiring the scenery when bullets kicked up the water just in front of me. My Corsair responded well to some violent turns and twists and I escaped. Several pilots did not return, however, two of them were from 1842 Squadron. Whilst waiting his turn to land one pilot ran out of fuel and ditched alongside the fleet. . . . We learned as we withdrew southwards that the *Tirpitz*, such a menace to Atlantic shipping, was disabled but not sunk. At least it was put out of action until it could be finished off by [Royal Air Force] Lancasters making their sortie from Russia.[3]

EQUIPPING THE FLEET AIR ARM

The FAA established an office in Washington, DC, on 1 October 1941 to coordinate further aircraft orders under the Lend-Lease act. Familiarity with the Grumman Martlet exposed the FAA to development of the F6F Hellcat and led to an initial order for 252 F6F-3s, with the first lot delivered in May 1943. Grumman did not stand up a second source for Hellcat production, electing to devote all of its wartime production to F6Fs, as second-source licensee General Motors took on production of Wildcats and Avengers. It quickly became clear to the FAA that U.S. Navy orders for Hellcats would far outstrip Grumman's ability to produce significant numbers for the Royal Navy. In short order, a lend-lease arrangement for Vought Corsairs was put in place.

The first of 95 F4U-1s, named Corsair Is in Royal Navy inventory, were delivered to an Admiralty delegation sited at Floyd Bennett Field in New York for further transshipment to Quonset Point, Rhode Island. In May 1943 Royal Navy pilots began conversion training on Corsairs at Quonset Point, the first cohort forming No. 1830 Naval Air Squadron. As greater numbers of pilots completed conversion training, Squadrons 1831, 1833, and 1834 formed. Training operations were expanded beyond Rhode Island to a newly opened naval air station at Brunswick, Maine. Training of FAA pilots in Corsairs began in earnest at Brunswick, utilizing auxiliary airfields at Lewiston, Sandford, and Rockland, Maine. By the end of 1943, eight full squadrons of FAA Corsairs were in commission, having completed their Corsair familiarization in New England.

The Royal Navy's Corsair Is were easily distinguishable by the birdcage canopies, stiff landing strut oleos, and pronounced wing drop in close. Corsair Is would never see operational duty on carriers but would serve primarily as conversion trainers. With a second tranche of Corsairs ordered from Vought out of F4U-1A production, framed bubble canopies began to appear; however, not all of the carrier suitability modifications were yet applied to the early production -1As. This group would be called Corsair IIs in FAA livery. Beginning with the -1As and continuing with subsequent Royal Navy versions of the Corsair, eight inches were clipped off left and right wing tips in order to clear the hangar deck entry overhead with wings in the folded position. Brewster-manufactured F3A-1Ds would enter Royal Navy inventory as Corsair IIIs, at 430 aircraft consuming slightly more than half of Brewster's entire Corsair production. Finally, 977 Goodyear-manufactured FG-1Ds, taken into inventory as Corsair IVs, brought the total number to 2,012.

Conversion training at Quonset Point amounted to familiarization with Corsair flying qualities, low-level navigation over open-ocean expanses, formation tactics, strafing practice, and field carrier landing practice. With conversion training completed, pilots and planes were taken aboard a CVE for transport to Britain. Pilot trainees were well aware of the Corsair's challenging habits in the landing pattern—several fatalities had occurred in the first weeks of simulated carrier landings. It was primarily in field carrier landing practice at

Quonset Point that Royal Navy pilots devised a modified approach to forestall the wing drop on final—surprisingly violent when it appeared. The standard approach involving a downwind leg opposite the ship's heading, flown to a 90-degree base leg, then through a 90-degree turn off the base leg to the final approach. This was deemed exceedingly difficult—in the first instance, for maintaining sight of the simulated flight deck through the turns, and in the second instance, for setting the pilot up for the left wing stall and wing drop in close followed by the dramatic bounce. Here, the Royal Navy pilots began flying a continuously circling turn, just above stalling speed, holding that speed all the way from the downwind leg to a point over the deck where the throttle would be cut, setting the airplane down on the deck. It seemed to work, at least for the Royal Navy.

When Nos. 1830 and 1833 returned to Britain with their airplanes as the first operational Corsair II squadrons, they would form into the 15th Naval Fighter Wing under the command of Lieutenant Commander Richard "Dicky" Cork for sea duty in HMS *Illustrious*. Dicky Cork was rated as an above-average pilot with ample experience, flying Skuas and Gladiators at sea in the first months of war with Germany. As the Battle of Britain began stretching Royal Air Force resources to the breaking point, FAA pilots were sought for shore-based fighter duty, and Cork was quick to volunteer. He flew Hurricanes on the wing of Squadron Leader Douglas Bader, a skilled pilot of some distinction in Britain, and later the United States. With Bader's unit, Cork scored five aerial victories before posting with a Martlet squadron that took him aboard HMS *Furious* for attacks on German-occupied installations and shipping in Norway. The squadron exchanged their Martlets for Sea Hurricanes and came aboard HMS *Indomitable* for Operation Pedestal near Malta. Dicky Cork scored another four aerial victories and two shared kills against German Ju-88s and Italian SM 79s.[4] He was on hand for the strikes on Tirpitz that prominently featured the combat debut of FAA Corsairs from *Illustrious*.

On the whole, German naval assets were reliably sidelined in Norwegian ports by 1944. That fact, and the surrender of Italy, relieved the Royal Navy for more far-flung duty. The focus for its big-deck carrier operations now shifted to the Indian Ocean, where the Japanese maintained an extensive footprint of airfields, ports, and oil refineries. Japan's relocation of large warships to Singapore that might complicate Central Pacific amphibious operations persuaded Admiral King to order USS *Saratoga* to the Indian Ocean to join *Illustrious* for raids on Japanese holdings to deny the Japanese unhindered access. Corsairs from *Illustrious* formed on Hellcats from *Saratoga* to cover strikes on Sabang, Sumatra, and Surabaya, Java. *Saratoga* was soon needed back in the Pacific and withdrew from the Indian Ocean area by May 1944. Grievously for the FAA, the much beloved Lieutenant Commander Dicky Cork perished in an accident near Ceylon shortly after. However, *Illustrious* was soon to enjoy the company of HMS *Victorious* with three Corsair II fighter squadrons—1834 with 19 Corsairs, and 1836 and 1838 with 18 each. To these two large-deck armored carriers was added a third, HMS *Indomitable*, with a Hellcat complement for its fighter squadron.

In October 1944 the U.S. Navy requested that the Royal Navy conduct a diversionary strike near the Nicobar Islands between the Bay of Bengal and the Andaman Sea to draw Japanese attention away from the U.S. landings in the Philippines. *Victorious* and *Indomitable* sailed for strikes on Nancowry Harbor. The attackers found their targets, but as the two carriers recovered aircraft and headed to open ocean with their escorts, a Japanese counterattack came on. *Indomitable*'s information network went down and did not detect the counterattack, and its combat air patrol of Hellcats failed to intercept. *Victorious* got her Corsairs into the air for the intercept when the Japanese were only 12 miles from the carriers. Nine Ki-43 Oscars at 7,000 feet and another three at 9,000 feet were engaged by the Corsairs. The Hellcats, late to the party, joined in. In a 40-minute melee, seven Oscars were shot down; however, two Corsairs from Squadron 1834 were lost, as was a Hellcat from *Indomitable*. Major Ronnie Hay aboard *Victorious*, impressed by the Corsairs' performance, was moved to observe: "The Corsair was just the right aircraft for that war. It was certainly better than anything we had, and an improvement on the Hellcat. It was more robust and faster, and although the Japanese could out-turn us in combat, we could out-climb, out-dive and out-gun him. By far the most healthy improvement was its endurance, as with about five hours' worth of fuel in your tanks you didn't have the agony of wondering whether or not you would make it back to the carrier."[5]

Corsairs of 1834 and 1836 Squadrons aboard HMS *Victorious*, fitted with extra fuel tanks, take position for launch to attack the Japanese maintenance and repair center at Sigli, Sumatra. (Imperial War Museum, London)

FAA ON ICEBERG'S LEFT FLANK

The excellent rapport between *Saratoga* and *Illustrious* notwithstanding, the role of the British carriers alongside the U.S. fleet in the Pacific campaigns of 1945 depended greatly on adapting to a common operating model between fleets. That required more synchronization and rehearsal than time permitted. There also was a fair amount of resistance to accommodating British carriers as a matter of political policy. A working compromise was reached on both counts. For Operation Iceberg, the taking of Okinawa, the British carriers were assigned the Sakishimas, a cluster of islands to the southwest of Okinawa proper. On each of the three major islands were three Japanese airfields from which kamikaze flights were expected to originate, threatening the left flank of Task Force 58 operating nearest Okinawa.

The FAA operated semi-independently in this secondary, albeit important, interdiction role, with substantial Corsair presence among their four big-deck carriers: HMS *Victorious* with 37 Corsairs split between No. 1834 and No. 1836 squadrons, HMS *Indefatigable* with an all-Seafire fighter contingent, HMS *Illustrious* with Squadrons 1830 and 1833 bringing 18 Corsairs each, and HMS *Formidable* with Squadrons 1841 and 1842, also with 18 Corsairs each. HMS *Indomitable* would join later in the Okinawa campaign with an all-Hellcat fighter force. The British carriers operated together as Task Force 57 departing Ulithi on 23 March to join Task Force 58 for Operation Iceberg.

On arrival, Task Force 57 was directed to strike airfields on Formosa, as this was deemed the more immediate source of Japanese reinforcements flown into Okinawa and kamikaze attacks on the amphibious force gathering around Okinawa. In addition to Formosa, a string of islands stretching northeasterly toward the main island of Okinawa harbored threatening airfields that had to be neutralized. The two main islands in that chain, Ishigaki and Miyako, each hosted three airstrips, with a seaplane base at Karimata on Miyako. The FAA proved up to the task, protecting the left flank of Task Force 58, which was wholly engaged in repulsing the aerial attacks coming down from Kyushu. In their first day on station as Task Force 57, *Victorious*'s

No. 1836 Corsairs were taking part in a fighter sweep over Miyako. Sub Lieutenant D. T. Chute, Royal Navy Volunteer Reserve, recalled, "A low-level approach was made until nearing Miyako Jima when the sweep climbed up to 8,000 feet and swept round to an up-sun position of Hirara airfield. Drop tanks were released and Green Flight followed Red Flight in a steep diving attack on the airfield from the north-east, opening fire at long range and closing to zero feet where it could be seen that the targets attacked were either dummies or damaged aircraft."[6]

Later that same day, four Corsairs on combat air patrol from *Victorious* encountered a Zeke kamikaze. Flight leader Lieutenant Commander Tommy Harrington wrote, "He was flying out of killing range and I carefully fired a good long blast over his port wing. He very kindly obliged by executing rather a difficult turn to port, which enabled me to close and shoot this unhappy amateur down."[7]

In the days that followed into April, operations from Task Force 57 settled into a routine. Target airstrips were revisited every two to three days to undo overnight repairs by Japanese construction crews filling bomb craters on runways. Typically, Corsairs would accompany Avengers, but those Japanese aircraft encountered near the target areas seemed much less interested in engaging to defend their airfields and more interested in heading directly to Task Force 57 surface units to attempt suicide attacks. Consistent but random kamikaze attacks became a regular daily exercise. On the day of *Yamato*'s sortie and attack by Task Force 58 airplanes north of Okinawa, Task Force 57 continued with fighter sweeps, called "Ramrods" by the British, on runways and airdrome facilities on the two main islands in the Sakishima chain. During a Ramrod by Corsairs from No. 1830 Squadron, one Corsair II drifted a little off the mark during a strafing run of buildings at Hirara. A Japanese round was seen to penetrate the Corsair's front windscreen and decapitate the pilot. Another Corsair was lost due to an oxygen tank failure and two more to accidents or mechanical failures. *Indefatigable* was struck by a Zeke kamikaze on the morning of the Okinawa landings, and a Tony kamikaze clipped *Illustrious* on 6 April. *Illustrious* was withdrawn, mainly due to the cumulative effects of many bomb hits earlier in the war. She was replaced on station by *Formidable*, which was subsequently hit several times by kamikazes. Her armored decks and bulkheads prevented extensive damage, permitting her to launch Corsair strikes on the Japanese home islands after Okinawa.

With Okinawa secured in late June, operations in July and August 1945 turned to stepped-up attacks on Japan. For the FAA, that included Corsair Squadrons 1834, 1836, 1841, and 1842 from *Victorious* and *Formidable*. On 9 August 1945, only six days before the Japanese surrender, Corsairs from Squadrons 1841 and 1842 *came down on* Shiogama harbor in the northern part of Honshu in a fighter sweep toward the Japanese naval base at Onagawa at the head of the harbor. Lieutenant Robert Hampton Gray, leading the division of Corsairs from No. 1841 Squadron, could see five Japanese warships at anchor. Anti-aircraft fire from ships in the harbor and from shore batteries intensified as the flight drew closer to their targets. Selecting a ship, *Amakusa*, Gray lined up for his run to deliver his 1,000-pound bomb. His Corsair was taking heavy flak hits. He suffered wounds and was losing control of the aircraft but pressed the attack to score a critical hit with his bomb release, sinking the destroyer. Gray was unable to pull out of the run and plunged into the bay. He would be the last Canadian killed in action in World War II and the only Royal Canadian Navy pilot to be awarded (posthumously) the Victoria Cross.[8]

NOTES

1. Michael Whitby, "Navy Blue Fighter Pilot," Vintage Wings of Canada, https://tomato-hibiscus-5kcf.squarespace.com/stories/donsheppardepisode2.

2. "Admiral C. W. Nimitz's Message to the Pacific Fleet," 2 September 1945, https://www.history.navy.mil/research/archives/digital-exhibits-highlights/vj-day/surrender/nimitz-message.html#:~:text=On%20board%20all%20naval%20vessels,1941%2C%20is%20at%20an%20end.

3. Martin W. Bowman, *The Men Who Flew the F4U Corsair* (Barnsley, UK: Pen & Sword Books, 2021), 135–36.

4. Bowman, *The Men Who Flew the F4U Corsair*, 124.

5. Hugh Popham, "The British Eastern Fleet," Armoured Aircraft Carriers of World War II, https://www.armouredcarriers.com/british-eastern-fleet-royal-navy-operations-in-the-indian-ocean.

6. Popham, "The British Eastern Fleet."

7. Popham, "The British Eastern Fleet."

8. Robert Hampton Gray, "Member Profile," Canada's Aviation Hall of Fame, 1974, https://cahf.ca/robert-hampton-gray/.

CORNCOB CORSAIRS

> Right after the gear doors closed, a P-51 went in, tearing off a wing and burning. Tony Jannezo, flying a Corsair, bought himself a plot in Marble Park on the Number Two pylon. This was followed by a P-51 going in on the backstretch, which was marked by the black smoke. Next a P-40Q buried itself in the Ohio countryside. This left the finishers: Cook Cleland in his F2G-1 Corsair, first; his second Corsair, flown by Dick Becker in second place.
>
> —Nick Rezich, "The 1947 Cleveland Air Races"[1]

THE WASP MAJOR

As early as 1940, days before the first flight of the XF4U-1 at Bridgeport Airport, Pratt & Whitney was making plans for a 3,000 hp air-cooled engine: this, a result of the impasse with U.S. Army Air Forces General Henry Arnold regarding Pratt's continued development of liquid-cooled engines. Intervention by Pratt's Frederick Rentschler had persuaded Arnold to back off his mandate for liquid cooling but with the implied commitment from Pratt & Whitney that they would keep developing more powerful radial designs. Internal studies began with three rows of nine-cylinder power sections (closest in design to the R-2800), four

The airframe differences between the F4U and the XF2G are shown in stark relief. (Smithsonian National Air and Space Museum)

rows of seven-cylinder power sections, and six rows of five-cylinder power sections. Design trades pointed to the power section with four rows of seven cylinders. Essentially, the chosen configuration was like placing two R-1830 engines in series with R-2800 cylinders but with each successive row indexed away from the first row's top cylinder to provide a twist in the cooling airflow. Trials on the test stand looked reasonably good. The first production R-4360–4 was shipped in January 1945 to Vultee in Downey, California, for integration into a prototype Model 72 Vengeance test craft to become the V-85. After an initial three-minute flight at Downey, it was shipped by flat-bed railcar to East Hartford, Connecticut, for more flight tests. Testing stopped in September 1942 when the aircraft was dead-sticked into a tobacco field. But word was slowly seeping out about this new colossal engine that was in development by Pratt.

Goodyear, licensed producer of the Corsair FG-1, was interested in the potential for this new engine to power one more upgrade to the Corsair. Wartime reports persuaded Goodyear executives that the Marine Corps, in particular, would appreciate the robust performance of a new R-4360–powered Corsair as a low-level high-speed interceptor but with even greater payload capability for ground attack. Goodyear maintained a design team that went to work fleshing out a preliminary configuration. Working from the FG-1 as their starting point, and in coordination with Pratt & Whitney for engine specifications and dimensional figures, they added a full 360-degree bubble canopy, more internal fuel, and a taller tail. In early 1944, Goodyear, with Vought's knowledge and approval, approached the Navy about its new F2G design. Goodyear marketing people dubbed their design the Super Corsair. Ultimately, BuAer officials took to calling the R-4360 the "Corncob Corsair" due to the engine's resemblance to a twisted corncob. The Navy responded very favorably to the design, ordering in March 1944 a prototype that would be based on the FG-1, plus 418 F2G-1s with manually folding wings, unequipped with tailhooks. With the Marine Corps order came an accompanying order for ten carrier-capable F2G-2s—a much smaller order because at the time, Corsairs had not yet been officially approved for operation from the aircraft carrier. When World War II ended with the Japanese surrender, only five examples of each type had been produced. Grumman's F8F Bearcat, already entering production, displayed comparable performance equipped with the same R-2800 engine that powered the F4U. And the Navy was down-selecting to fewer types. Further production of F2Gs was canceled. The

The XF2G-1 prototype delivered to the test center at Patuxent River. (NARA)

Cook Cleland's 1946 entry in the Thompson Trophy race: a highly modified FG-1 that he named "Lucky Gallon." (Alamy)

Cleland's 1947 racing team enjoyed support from Vought, Goodyear, and Pratt & Whitney. Racing team members from all three companies are shown in this group image, with Cook Cleland on the far left. (Alamy)

ten that had been produced were consigned to deep storage awaiting an eventual order that they be broken up for scrap.

CORNCOB RACERS

Lieutenant Commander "Cook" Cleland had established an impressive wartime record—but as a dive-bomber pilot of SB2Us and SBDs, not in the cockpit of the F4U. In the early days of the Guadalcanal campaign, he bombed Japanese guns on Tulagi into silence and went swimming in shark-infested waters when his ship, USS *Wasp*, was torpedoed and sunk. He became a plank-owner in a newly formed SBD squadron, VB-16, in USS *Lexington*. He flew in the first Battle of the Philippine Sea, and for his direct hit on the Japanese carrier *Junyo* was presented the Navy Cross. He finished the war in command of an SB2C dive-bomber squadron making attacks on the Japanese home islands. With war's end, he discovered that tutoring new flight students in Piper Cubs as a fixed base operator in Willoughby, Ohio, did not provide the excitement he needed. He remembered the feeling of being enthralled at a young age by the air racers of that earlier time, and with no prospect of flying Navy aircraft in his immediate future, he determined to jump into air racing.

This was a time when war surplus fighter aircraft were a glut on the open commercial market. The National Air Races in Cleveland, suspended during the war years, restarted in 1946 and would be dominated by highly modified warbirds. On his own, Cleland bought a surplus Goodyear-produced FG-1 Corsair and modified it to lighten the gross weight; he named it "Lucky Gallon." Entering the 1946 National Air Race, he finished sixth with an average speed of 357 mph over a closed-circuit 15-mile course of 20 laps. What he quickly realized was that his FG-1 was outclassed by surplus P-51s and P-38s modified for greater speed. Ironically, the winner of the Thompson Trophy for first place in that 1946 competition was a highly prepped P-63 Cobra, a distant relative of the Bell Airacobra that the XF4U-1 had bested in the Navy fighter competition before the war.

Cleland made up his mind to parlay with someone who could help. As it happened, Fleet Admiral Bull Halsey was in attendance at the 1946 race and was heard to quip that it would sure be nice if some Navy guy could win. Cleland traded on his name recognition as one of the racers to secure an appointment with Halsey. As the story goes, there was an instant rapport and a meeting of the minds. Halsey did not have to be persuaded by Cleland's remarks that the air races were national in scope and that great prestige accrued to the military service that placed high in the finish. Halsey's interest was roused. He asked Cleland what it would take for the Navy to win, and without hesitation, Cleland answered, "the Corncob Corsair." The F2Gs locked up in storage had to be released for public sale. And so it happened that a surplus F2G came on the military equipment market, and Cleland was first in line to pay $1,250 for a surplus F2G to be picked up at Naval Air Station Jacksonville, Florida. Before the 1947 race, Cleland picked up two other F2Gs from war surplus assets.

Cleland's small team went to work on the Super Corsairs, removing avionics, tailhooks, and wingfold mechanisms. Special scoops were applied to take in more cooling ram air, and a 100-gallon water injection system was installed. Articulating flaps were eliminated and made part of the wing to get smoother uninterrupted airflow. Hamilton Standard provided thin-blade propellers. Finally, Vought Aircraft Company came onboard to provide more than 6,000 hours of technical support and to finish the F2G racers in an eye-catching high-gloss paint scheme. To ensure that Cleland's aircraft was easily identifiable among a crowded field of 13 entrants, his F2G was painted with a large number 74 on the cowl. His other F2G team entrants bore numbers 84 and 94.

THOMPSON TROPHY WINNER

The preparation paid off. The basic F4U design now powered by the colossal Wasp Major engine asserted its dominance. Cleland won the National Air Race of 1947 and the Thompson Trophy by recording an average speed over the race of 396.13 mph. The 15-mile closed course was laid out as a square that had to be cornered four times at seven Gs, meaning that Cleland was clocking close to 500 mph on the straightaways. And to complete the day, Cleland's team pilot, Dick Becker, finished in second place with F2G number 94, bringing their team winnings for race day to $27,900. A third team pilot, Tony Jannezo, was overcome after the first eight laps of the race by carbon monoxide fumes penetrating his cockpit and regrettably died in the crash.

Despite several tragic accidents during the 1949 Thompson Trophy race, or perhaps partly because of the elimination of such stiff competition, Cook Cleland's F2G Corsairs finished first, second, and third. Cook led the field over the finish in number 94. Evident in this image as Cook peers into the cockpit are the clipped wings that provided some margin of speed. (Alamy)

Cleland entered the 1948 National Air Race, hoping to repeat his win the year before. To his dismay, engine failure in the fourth lap forced him out early. He committed then to entering and winning the 1949 race. He knew competition was stiffening; other entrants were trying out new fuel mixtures and lightened materials. Cleland explored a fuel mixture called menthol triptane with a 240+ octane rating, and he began using water injection composed of hydrogen peroxide. He cut off 4.5 feet from each outer wing, adding wing end plates. On advice from Hamilton Standard, he added a spinner to the prop hub. With these changes, he was able to eke out another 12 mph in test runs. With the race finally started, he led the entire field the whole distance, actually throttling back in the last lap to preserve the engine. Cleland won his second Thompson Trophy in the F2G and set a new world speed record doing it.

Cleland was only the second multi-time winner in National Air Race history after Roscoe Turner's three wins, his last in 1939. But another war loomed just over the horizon. Cleland had maintained his Naval Reserve affiliation as the commanding officer of a reserve Corsair squadron. When naval aviation surged for the Korean War, his unit was called to active duty. Racing was now a trifle to put behind him as he took his squadron of F4U-4Bs aboard USS *Valley Forge* for her third war cruise in October 1951. The action was intense, little different from what he experienced in the last war but without the expectation of battling large enemy aircraft formations at sea. Cleland's Corsair was brought down by communist ground fire in May 1952. He was rescued the same day and lived to retire from the Navy in 1967.

NOTE

1. Nick Rezich, "The 1947 Cleveland Air Races," *Vintage Airplane* 33, no. 7 (2005): 4–6.

CORSAIR ENCORE

Lieutenant Commander Tom Blackburn of VF-17 would remember 25 January 1944 as a day of surpassing importance. The night before, he led VF-17 to their new base at Torokina, Bougainville. That morning he learned that they would escort their first strike from their new fighter strip at Piva Yoke the following day. It would be a maximum effort requiring 32 Corsairs, nearly the entire VF-17 complement. And for VF-17 it would be the first attack on Rabaul.

On that very day, halfway around the globe in Stratford, Connecticut, Vought Aircraft received the Navy's letter of intent to proceed with the newest Corsair configuration, the F4U-4. The first F4U-1D had not yet been towed out of final assembly, but the Navy was already looking for a new and improved Corsair that would fly and climb faster, higher, and farther. Despite diminishing production capacity, the Japanese were turning out a new generation of fighters that excelled over the earlier A6M Zekes typically encountered from the Solomons to the Marianas. The Nakajima Ki-84 Frank, Kawanishi N1K2 George, and Horikoshi-designed Mitsubishi J2M Jack were beginning to close the performance

In the closing days of World War II, Lieutenant John Glenn of VMF-155 flies an F4U-4 on a strike mission to reduce bypassed Japanese holdouts in the Marshall Islands. (Smithsonian National Air and Space Museum)

advantage held by the F4U-1D. To restore the Corsair's advantage, more capability was the order of the day. Production of F4U-1D and Goodyear FG-1D would total 3,682, on top of 2,814 F4U-1s and -1As already delivered by Vought and 2,745 FG-1s and F3A-1s from Goodyear and Brewster. The F4U-4, produced only by Vought, however, amounted to the first major step increase in Corsair performance and "habitability."

F4U-4 RAISES THE ANTE

Vought's engineering development staff was continually fine-tuning the Corsair to eke out even greater performance. After more than a year of combat in the Solomons, pilot feedback pointed to a number of ergonomic or "creature comfort" changes for improved cockpit efficiency and reduced pilot workload. Working hand in hand with Pratt & Whitney and Hamilton Standard, the Vought team created the much-anticipated and clearly visible permutation to the basic Corsair with incorporation of the 2800–18W. This variant of the power plant produced 2,450 hp at war emergency power, upping the Corsair's top speed at 26,000 feet to 450 mph from the -1D's 425 mph at 20,000 feet. Its expected rate of climb of more than 4,000 feet per minute and extended service ceiling at 41,000 feet rendered eye-opening performance when compared side by side with earlier F4U models.[1] The -18W used liquid couplings for the auxiliary stage, eliminating the "solid" drive via gears and clutches. Externally, one could discern the addition of a scoop on the lower cowl lip that now channeled air for an auxiliary stage blower air, with larger oil coolers and intercoolers. Around the engine mount, cowl flaps were reduced from 15 to 5 on each side, with a single hydraulic actuating strut at the bottom of the cowl, precluding oil smear on the windshield. And a four-bladed Hydromatic propeller with wide-faired blade shanks evoked a more powerful, menacing Corsair. Two F4U-1As nearing completion were detoured from final assembly to receive the essential -18W and propeller changes, designated F4U-4Xs. Boone Guyton took the first of the -4Xs up for its test flight on 19 April 1944 and noted, in his matter-of-fact manner, that the increased performance was exhilarating. The new engine and proven gull-winged airframe exceeded all projections. Vought had another winner.

As flight-testing got underway to assess the flight performance resulting from the power plant changes, five more prototypes, designated XF4U-4s, incorporated the "habitability" and pilot workload improvements. Inside the cockpit, every effort was made by the Vought engineers to ease the task load on the pilot:

- Engine controls were rearranged to provide for single power lever control movement throughout the range of climb and level flight (in the F4U-1, throttle and prop were remote from each other; in the F4U-4, it was now possible to grasp and move both simultaneously). An anti-creep friction lock was added to hold throttle and prop throughout catapult stroke on the flight deck. And manually controlled hydraulic valves for oil cooler air and intercooler air exit flaps were made automatic for secondary engine controls.
- A thumb latch was integrated onto the throttle for war emergency power water injection, replacing safety wires across the throttle quadrant and thereby preventing inadvertent actuation.
- The raised tail wheel had the unintended effect of making pilot entry up to the cockpit more cumbersome. To address that, the right-hand inboard center section flap was now used as a step, with an interconnect between the large double step on the left side of the fuselage and wing flap control that permitted lowering the flaps from the ground for easier access to that first step. The additional step and handgrip on the left side of the fuselage allowed a mechanic to make a hurried exit when the pilot came up the right-hand side in a scramble. And the flap step eliminated the wing walkway cover, with an accompanying drag reduction that equated to 3 mph in up-and-away flight.
- The cockpit deck was raised to eliminate the "deep pit" effect and to raise the pilot's legs to aid in G resistance during hard maneuvering.
- The improved "clear vision" canopy that removed the metal reinforcing strips over the top, appearing in later F4U-1s, was now made a standard on F4U-4s.
- The control stick was shortened by raising its pivot point 18 inches without changing its movement as measured at the top of the stick. The increased angular travel of the stick gave greater advantage in hard-over stick maneuvers, minimizing interference with the pilot's thighs.

- Rudder pedals were suspended 10 inches higher from a crossbeam forward of the instrument panel for greater pilot comfort and maintenance access. The resulting six inches more travel could better accommodate different leg lengths and positions.
- The chart board was moved to a rack to the right of the pilot's seat, held by a single spring-loaded latch, which allowed better grouping of flight engine instruments on the cockpit panel.

A frequent gripe from pilots was the difficulty in adjusting the seat back and its armor plating when wearing a parachute pack slung under the pilot's backside. The F4U-1 seat with integral seat back was replaced by a seat pan with one-quarter-inch armor plate that tilted as it raised through four inches of adjustment. This permitted the pilot to adjust the angle of his pack at will by hitching forward or back. The seat back was now a separate slab of three-eighths-inch armor for maximum protection. Mounted on the back plate was a revised shoulder harness using a spring-wound cable reel allowing 18 inches of adjustment with lock holes every half-inch of travel. That was a profound change from the F4U-1's sliding tube and scant inches of available adjustment.

The first production F4U-4 flew in September 1944, and a spin-off configuration with 20-mm cannons in lieu of .50-caliber guns, the F4U-4B, was put into production for 297 copies. Corsair production that had been humming at well over 250 aircraft per month now slowed to 118 with the changeover to the -4. By May 1945, though, 302 F4U-4s had rolled off assembly for acceptance tests. Production had fully recovered and now exceeded earlier rates, up to 300 in June and July. The first F4U-4s reached the western Pacific theater by summer, too late to make any meaningful contribution to the war, which ended on 15 August. For Vought, the pace slackened immediately. By September production of all F4U-4s was reduced to 41 airplanes and down to just 21 by December. But then, in February 1946, the Navy gave Vought new hope in an era of steep naval aviation downsizing. Another letter of intent—again, based on a proposal from the Vought development engineers—authorized the company to proceed with the F4U-5 version of the Corsair. A decision near the end of the war to retain the Corsair as the more capable fighter-bomber ensured that the F6F-5 Hellcat would disappear from flight decks by 1948, replaced briefly by the F8F Bearcat. The Corsair would fly on. To safeguard Corsair production capacity, and to extract the most capability from the airplane as engines advanced, the prudent course was to develop the F4U-5 with the new 2800–32W engine. Where the -4 configuration had most to do with harnessing the 2800–18W engine and with serviceability and pilot ergonomics, the -5 design would have everything to do with leveraging the 2800–32W for enhanced mission effectiveness.

F4U-5: APEX OF CORSAIR COMBAT UTILITY

As with the F4U-4, the centerpiece of the F4U-5 modification was the upgrade to the power plant, taking the Pratt & Whitney R-2800 to the -32W series. The engine produced 200 hp more than the -18W on takeoff and maintained greater power to a higher altitude. The F4U-5 was now projected to clock slightly in excess of 470 mph at 26,800 feet, and was thought to be able to fight at 45,000 feet. Dual impellers arranged in parallel to pump auxiliary stage air were mounted 90 degrees about the engine's longitudinal axis, prompting the "Sidewinder" nickname for the -32W mount. The -5 design added automatic cowl flaps, intercooler flaps, and oil cooler doors, and relocated the air inlet from the six o'clock position on the lower cowl lip to separate inlets at the four o'clock and eight o'clock positions on the cowl. The four-blade prop was retained but with thinner blade tips to accommodate higher speeds and a reinforced hub to reduce the stresses brought on by drooping the thrust axis by three degrees for greater longitudinal stability. Finally, outer wing panels were made all metal in lieu of a combination of wood and fabric.

Pilot ergonomics were not forgotten. Automatic power control eliminated the need for a supercharger control lever on the pilot's throttle quadrant. High-speed maneuverability was enhanced with spring tabs for elevator and rudder control, decreasing control forces required of the pilot by 40 percent at high speed compared to the F4U-4. The tailhook lever was relocated to the right-hand side of the cockpit to be consistent with Navy cockpit panel recommendations. And a more highly bulged, power-actuated canopy was raised slightly for even better pilot vision, while inside the cockpit, folding armrests were provided. Maintenance access to the radio compartment was made easier with a door installed on the right-hand side of the fuselage two feet behind the trailing edge flap on the wing stub.

Yet the -5 was all about mission effectiveness. In lieu of .50-caliber guns, 20-mm guns were made standard with 924 rounds of ammunition. However, the -5 would be the first Corsair to be completely equipped with the lead-computing Mk 6 gunsight that included rocket-aiming provisions, with gunfire controlled by a ranging twist-type throttle grip. The centerline bomb rack similar to what Charles Lindbergh had tinkered with during his wartime Pacific sojourn was now made standard and capable of a 2,000-pound bomb load. And, of course, the two stub wing racks could still carry 1,000 pounders each. Finally, the wings supported eight Mk 9 rocket launchers for 3.5-inch or 5-inch high velocity aircraft–type rockets. To aid in getting a potential 5,000-pound ordnance load off the flight deck, catapult hooks were repositioned forward to permit catapult shots at the higher gross weights.

PERFORMANCE ENOUGH FOR MUSCULAR MISSION VARIANTS

Navy interest in specialty mission configurations figured prominently in the introduction of the F4U-5. In addition to 223 day-fighter F4U-5s and 30 F4U-5P photo birds, 315 night-fighter F4U-5N versions were produced. F4U-5Ps could accommodate K-17 or K-18 cameras in rotating mounts or S-7S continuous strip cameras. Cameras were mounted several feet behind and below the pilot's seat. All photoreconnaissance F4U-5Ps featured one vertical and two oblique sliding camera doors installed on the lower fuselage about four feet behind the trailing edge of the stub wing, with an oil deflector for each of the doors. In the cockpit, lighting control switches were placed on the forward right-hand console, camera control panel on the mid-right-hand console. For the strip camera, the power and film speed controller was mounted on the glare shield to the right of the gunsight, and for the K-series camera, an intervalometer timing unit that automatically tripped the camera shutter at predetermined intervals was located at the same spot on the glare shield.

The F4U-5N featured prominently the AN/APS-19 search radar, with scanner and receiver-transmitter mounted in an under-slung nacelle on the right-hand outer wing panel and radar scope in the upper center of the cockpit instrument panel, giving it much the same outward and inward appearance as the earlier

F4U-5N Corsair night-fighter with drop tank. (Smithsonian National Air and Space Museum)

Captain David Booker, USMC, mans an F4U-5P on board USS *Valley Forge* in July 1950. The camera window is clearly visible beneath the U.S. insignia. (NHHC)

F4U-2 with APS-4 mount. The -5N also provided an automatic pilot with control—a toggle-type switch and pressure knob—mounted on the right-hand console within easy reach. The autopilot could be disengaged by either control stick forces or manual de-clutching with a switch on the left-hand console. The Mk 6 gunsight, standard in the F4U-5, was replaced by the Mk 20 illuminated sight with night-fighter reticle. If the pilot's night vision through the windscreen became clouded by oil or grime, a system was installed to spray degreasing fluid over the windscreen at the touch of a button under the glare shield. To prevent momentary flash blindness, flash hiders obscured the muzzle flash from the pilot's visual scan. And flame hiders obscured the exhaust stack fire from the pilot's scan. For operation in very cold climates, 101 of 315 night-fighters were winterized as -5NLs, adding deicing boots on wings and tail, as well as deice shoes on the propeller blades.[2]

POSTWAR TRANSITIONS

Vought's pattern was to prototype a new series by leveraging the producibility baked into the baseline model or prior Corsair series design. This was the case again for the F4U-5, where two F4U-4 aircraft were inducted as the starting point for prototype construction, with one F4U-4B bearing 20-mm guns inducted as a third prototype.[3] The usual teething problems with engine-airframe integration for new variants did not slow down the prototype flight-testing appreciably, such that the first production F4U-5s flew in October 1947.

That year, another first flight took place that signaled broader and more significant changes to naval aviation that also augured a sunset for the Corsair. The XF9F-2 took flight at Grumman's Bethpage, New York, site. By June 1950, Navy-wide, six fighter squadrons were equipped with F9F Panthers and two with jet-powered McDonnell-produced F2H Banshees. In the Pacific Fleet, three carriers hosted jet fighter squadrons, USS *Boxer* (CV-21), USS *Valley Forge* (CV-45), and USS *Philippine Sea* (CV-47).[4] At that time, their air groups were typically made up of two jet fighter squadrons (F9F-2 or -3 Panthers, or F2H Banshees), one or two prop fighter squadrons (F4U-4 or F4U-5 Corsairs), one prop attack squadron (AD-4 Skyraiders), and various specialty missions including F4U-5N or F4U-5P detachments. Overall, the drawdown in fleet carrier strength since the end of World War II had been dramatic, with only 11 in commission at the start of 1950 from 28 in 1945.[5] In June, events would find the only one of the 11 carriers that was available and close to need was *Valley Forge*. From *Valley Forge*'s air group, the Corsair's combat utility would again be called upon to stem a new threat.

U-BIRDS OVER KOREA

Freshly installed Soviet puppet Supreme Leader Kim Il Sung of North Korea, apparently of his own volition but with Soviet and Communist Chinese acquiescence, launched nine infantry divisions and an armored division to spearhead an attack into South Korea across the 38th parallel on 25 June 1950. U.S. forces, caught unaware and unprepared, were pushed back behind a small salient in a corner of South Korea defined as the Pusan Perimeter. As fast-moving Communist forces overran their air bases, Air Force tactical fighters and bombers were quickly denied an operating footprint in Korea and were forced to fly into Korea from bases in Japan.

Lieutenant J. O. Harless of VF-94 was unable to return with his F4U-4 to USS *Philippine Sea* (CVA-47) due to battle damage, instead diverting to K-18 airfield. He crash-landed and suffered serious head wounds. Here, a flight line mechanic sits in the airplane waiting for the tow tractor. (Courtesy of Jeffrey Ethell Collection)

The only fleet carrier in the western Pacific area, USS *Valley Forge*, got underway from Hong Kong and steamed north by way of the Philippines to take position off South Korea. U.S. leaders discussed how to best slow the North Korean advance, and high priority was accorded strikes around the capital city of Pyongyang to include airfields, rail concentrations, and bridges. Authorization to hit these areas was passed to *Valley Forge*, with the addition of rail facilities and tracks along a north-south axis running through Kumshon, Sariwon, and Sinanju. On 3 July Air Group Five in *Valley Forge* off South Korea's west coast launched 12 Skyraiders and 16 F4U-4s, followed by the F9F Panthers that flew ahead to sweep the area clear of any aerial opposition and to suppress anti-aircraft fire. That strike organization was repeated twice a day roughly every other day in July, with VF-53 and VF-54 providing eight F4U-4Bs each for strikes on definite, preplanned targets. For controlled close support operations aiding troops in contact, four separate launches of three hours each were scheduled for eight F4U-4Bs from each Corsair squadron, accompanied by eight-plane Panther sweeps ahead of each Corsair launch to maintain coverage for most of the daylight hours. With fixed site targets, Corsairs obtained moderate success against tunnels and bridge abutments by skip-bombing or masthead attacks using 2,000-pound bombs with a 4- to 5-second fusing delay. Wartime operating conditions revealed that more armor plating was desired for Corsairs doing extensive close support work.[6]

In August, reinforcements caught up. *Philippine Sea* joined *Valley Forge* with two F4U-4B squadrons, Air Group 11's VF-113 and VF-114. Two CVEs arrived with *Philippine Sea*, USS *Badoeng Strait* (CVE-116) and USS *Sicily* (CVE-118). Two more F4U-4B squadrons were added with VMF-214 operating from *Sicily* and VMF-323 in *Badoeng Strait*. VMF-214 Corsairs launched in the late afternoon of 3 August to strike Chinju and

the village of Sinbanni, recently overrun by North Korean forces. Using incendiary bombs, rockets, and numerous strafing runs, the first evidence of serious opposition took the North Korean troops by surprise. On the following day, more strikes were flown to take pressure off the Eighth Army southern flank. These strikes hit bridges, railroads, and troop concentrations in the Chinju and Sacheon areas. VMF-323 Corsairs from *Badoeng Strait* entered the fray on 6 August with strikes west of Chinju along the Nam River, using 5-inch rockets and 500-pound bombs on structures that were concealing concentrations of North Korean infantry. The carriers were able to cruise near the Pusan perimeter and give the Marine Corsairs access to a full menu of targets without being overly concerned with range or time to the target. In an early and fruitful demonstration of joint operations with the Air Force, VMF-323 on 11 August, teamed up with F-51 Mustangs near Kosong to execute the so-called Kosong Turkey Shoot. With assistance from the F-51s, Marine F4U-4Bs hit a North Korean motorized regiment convoy of command vehicles, light armor, and infantry trucks, and flattened every one of 100 vehicles. Corsairs of VMF-214 and -323 became a constant daytime presence over the front line, orbiting while waiting for calls for ground attack to relieve pressure from advancing Communist troops. In the evening, during hours of darkness, F4U-5Ns of VMF(N)-513 commuted in from Itazuke airfield on Kyushu to knock down hecklers.[7]

Ensign Robert Horton, in his first tour with VF-113 from *Philippine Sea*, recalled a mission on 13 August that was his first under enemy fire:

> We were ordered to destroy the Rising Sun Oil Refinery, located within the city of Pyongyang and it was heavily defended with a ring of anti-aircraft batteries. My Corsair was armed with a 500-pound bomb, eight 5-inch [high-velocity aircraft rockets], plus 900 rounds of 20-mm ammunition. During my first bombing run, the [anti-aircraft artillery] was so thick you could walk on it. I figured that

Lieutenant Don Engen test-flies the last production AU-1 in September 1952 as the Bureau of Aeronautics acceptance pilot attached to the Naval Industrial Reserve Plant office in Grand Prairie, Texas. Engen would rise to three-star rank and in retirement become the director of the Smithsonian National Air and Space Museum. (Smithsonian National Air and Space Museum)

if the pilots ahead of me could make their bomb runs with little or no apparent damage, I could too! I made a perfect run and did some strafing as we pulled back to the carrier. To my shock when I climbed out of the cockpit, I discovered I had forgotten to arm my bomb because the arming wire was missing, which meant the bomb probably hit the target but did not explode. More than likely, that unexploded bomb caused some psychological problems for anyone that was working close to it! Later, the weather turned cold and there was snow up close to the Yalu. We found a bunch of enemy troops in the snow and they were apparently playing dead. After communicating with one of our Skyraider pilots, we decided that he would dive on them first and release his two napalm bombs and I would follow right behind with my 20-mm [cannons]. When those troops saw the napalm release, they jumped up and started running straight into my 20-mm fire. We did receive a lot of small arms fire on those passes and when I returned to the carrier, my Corsair had quite a few small holes in it. Every one of the missions we flew up north was dangerous because of the intense ground fire. When the Chinese came in, they brought a lot more high-caliber weapons in an effort to protect their supply convoys.[8]

One month later, United Nations forces landed at Inchon, with an initial objective of retaking the air base at Kimpo. Corsairs of VMF-214 and VMF-323 supported the landings from CVE flight decks. As soon as the air base was secured, VMF-212 and VMF-312 Corsairs arrived for basing ashore at Kimpo. From the four Marine Corsair fighter squadrons, 2,163 ground attack sorties were flown over 33 days to clear opposition on the ground for the Marines' movement inland.[9] In time, the dual role of fighter and bomber Corsair employment prompted a name change for some Marine Corsair fighter squadrons from VMF to Marine Attack Squadrons (VMAs). VMFs-212, -312, -332, and 332 were relabeled VMAs. Equipment was changing as well. Squadrons flying F4U-4s switched to F4U-4Bs to enhance the ground attack role with more throw-weight in strafing runs. A more discernable change appeared when VMA-212 and VMA-323 introduced the last in the series of Corsairs to serve in U.S. colors: the AU-1.

The Marine Corps looked to Vought as the Korean War got underway, to optimize the Corsair for a high-intensity ground attack role. Yet another derivative of the R-2800 engine, the 83W, was chosen as the baseline power plant, with oil coolers moved inboard to provide greater protection from ground fire. Top speed actually slowed despite the added horsepower due to the additional armor plate that was requested. The F4U-5 was the starting point for prototyping as the XF4U-6 soon changed to AU-1 in production. The AU-1 retained the four 20-mm cannons but added two more under-wing racks for stores, with production running to 111 aircraft.

CORSAIR MiG KILLER

With the tide of land warfare in Korea seemingly very fluid and ramp space at a premium, VMA-312 moved offshore to operate from USS *Sicily*. The squadron was scheduled for yet another interdiction mission on 10 September 1952 and launched a large number of F4U-4Bs against a troop concentration near Chinnampo near the mouth of the Taedong River. Captain Jesse G. Folmar was leading a four-plane division when the flight arrived at the target area. He remembered what happened next:

As we started to bank over a small island off the coast, I caught a glimpse of two MiG-15s in the early stages of setting up for firing pass on us. They were in loose section formation, so I steepened the angle of my banking turn into them, while at the same time increasing power. I jettisoned all external ordnance and fuel tanks and then switched to the guard channel to report that we were being attacked by MiGs. Seconds later, I spotted two more of them closing rapidly from my "eight o'clock." I turned hard to the left, trying to bring my guns to bear before they could open fire, but due to their rapid closure, I was unable do so. Their tracers were overshooting us, so I reversed my bank to the right and turned inside one of the MiGs as he started a climbing left turn. I pulled up and got him squarely in my gunsights, giving him about 20 mils' lead. I then triggered off a long five-second burst with my four 20-mm cannon. I could tell that I had him boresighted by the blinking flashes along the left side of his fuselage. A grey trail of fuel vapor began to stream from the MiG, and this quickly turned into billowing black smoke. He nosed over slightly and seemed to lose acceleration. Seconds later the pilot ejected, and he tumbled through the air in what appeared to be a ball of smoke. When his parachute opened, I could see his G suit burning from head to foot. I glanced down and saw the flaming MiG hit the water vertically. . . . Soon four more MiGs joined the fight, strung out in a loose column of two sections. I had just started picking up good diving speed when I saw balls of tracer passing on my left. At that instant I felt a severe jolt and explosion in my left wing. My aircraft began to shudder as if in a high-speed stall. I glanced over and saw that my left aileron and about four feet of my left wing were gone. Also, the top of the left wing was gutted to the inboard side of my inboard 20-mm gun. My airplane was trying to roll to the left, although the control column was placed in a full right position. This led to my decision that it would be too hazardous to attempt a landing back on *Sicily*, so I decided to bail out.[10]

KOREAN WAR CORSAIR ACE

Carrier air group composition remained relatively stable throughout the Korean War. However, the disparity in performance between jets and props required due consideration in the launch and recovery process. The fleet carriers operated a 1.5-hour cycle time—launch to recovery—for the F9F Panthers, and a 3-hour double cycle for the props. The Skyraiders could manage the double cycle time on internal fuel, but the Corsairs—without as much internal fuel—normally needed to carry a drop tank to comfortably orbit the ship at mission's end waiting for a recovery time.[11] The drop tank became part of the standard load-out for the Corsair that typically included full ammunition and, for ground support work, a 150-gallon napalm tank and six 100-pound general purpose bombs. For taking down bridge spans, the payload changed to one 500-pound general purpose bomb and six 100-pounders, or alternatively one 1,000-pound bomb and four 100-pound bombs, with 5-inch high-velocity aircraft rockets or 11.75-inch Tiny Tim rockets for reinforced structural piers or abutments footing bridges.[12]

Straight-wing jets and prop-driven Corsairs did not measure up to the performance of the MiG-15, so aerial combat reminiscent of the prior war over the South Pacific was not the order of the day. Carrier air group missions over the beach in Korea were focused on interdiction or close air support. Jet fighters, owing to their higher speed, showed best as flak suppressors and target combat air patrol. Skyraiders could carry the heaviest bomb loads in to the target. Corsairs proved to be the best all-around workhorse for their versatility at carrying heavy ordnance loads and for their speed and maneuverability in the target area. This versatility was recognized when, early in the war, Air Group Two

Cook Cleland, winner of the Thompson Trophy in 1949 in a F2G Super Corsair, commanded VF-653 in USS *Valley Forge* upon his recall to active duty. Here, one of his squadron's F4U-4Bs starts a deck run for takeoff to join a strike mission over Korea in May 1952. (Courtesy of Jeffrey Ethell Collection)

Lieutenant Guy Bordelon gazes at the nose art of his F4U-5N, an homage to his wife. In that aircraft, he scored his fifth aerial victory on 17 July 1952 to become the Navy's first and only Corsair ace of the Korean War. (NARA)

deployed with only F4U-4 fighter squadrons: in USS *Boxer* in August 1950 with four Corsair fighter squadrons totaling 64 aircraft (no jets), again in USS *Valley Forge* for her second combat cruise (no jets), and a third time with USS *Philippine Sea* on her second combat deployment in March 1951 (no jets). These deployments yielded some laudatory Corsair achievements. For the crucial first 10 months of the Korean War, F4Us accounted for 82 percent of all close support missions flown by Navy and Marine pilots.

Even as the photographic-reconnaissance mission was transitioning to F9F-2P or F2H-2P jet aircraft at the start of the war, invariably, the night-fighting mission remained the domain of the F4U-5N and the winterized -5NL. Night-fighter detachments from Composite Squadron Three served in every air group throughout the Korean War. One night-fighter would gain fleet-wide notice in the summer of 1953.

It began when the Air Force at Kimpo air base determined they had had enough of the nightly harassing flights by droning North Korean propeller aircraft. The risk they had to consider was the possibility that these obsolete trainers could drop a bomb onto a tarmac area densely packed with F-86s undergoing overnight maintenance. A call was made to USS *Princeton* operating offshore for temporary assignment of night-fighters at Kimpo to deal with the hecklers. F4U-5Ns from Air Group Fifteen's VC-3 Detachment Delta arrived at Pyongtaek south of Seoul and began nightly patrols. Between 30 June and 16 July 1953, Lieutenant Guy P. Bordelon, one of the night-fighter Corsair pilots leading the *Princeton* detachment, scored shootdowns of two Yak-18s, two Po-2 trainer types, and finally, on 16 July, a third Po-2. With his fifth kill, Bordelon became an ace, the only Navy ace of the Korean War, and was presented the Navy Cross.

NOTES

1. Guyton, *Whistling Death*, 184, 187.

2. Bert Kinzey, *F4U Corsair in Detail & Scale, Part 2: F4U-4 through F4U-7* (Carrollton, TX: Squadron/Signal, 1998), 49.

3. D'Angina, *Vought F4U Corsair*, 33.

4. Francillon, *Grumman Aircraft*, 324.

5. "U.S. Ship Force Levels," Naval History and Heritage Command, https://www.history.navy.mil/resesarch/histories/ship-histories/us-ship-force-levels.html.

6. H. P. Lanham, Operations Report, Ser. 059-50, 2 August 1950, http://www.koreanwar-educator.org/topics/Reports/after_action/korean_combat_action_reports_for_carrier_air_group_5.pdf.

7. John Condon and Peter Mersky, *Corsairs to Panthers* (Washington, DC: CreateSpace Independent Publishing, 2002), 7.

8. Warren Thompson, *Naval Aviation in the Korean War* (Barnsley, UK: Pen & Sword Aviation, 2012), 26–27.

9. Peter B. Mersky, *U.S. Marine Corps Aviation since 1912* (Annapolis, MD: Naval Institute Press, 2009), 126.

10. Jesse G. Folmar, in Warren Thompson, *F4U Units of the Korean War* (Oxford: Osprey Publishing, 2012).

11. Thompson, *F4U Units of the Korean War*, 64.

12. Thompson, *F4U Units of the Korean War*, 60.

THE BENT-WING FLIES ON

For the experienced pilots of the "Royale" [the French navy], this legendary aircraft, which had already won glory in the Pacific War, was an unforgettable adventure. From Bach Maï to Bizerte, via Suez and Algeria, the AU-1 and F4U-7 proved their formidable efficiency. The "Corsairs" of the Republic have made France proud.

—Patrick Marchand and Junko Takamori, *Les Ailes de Gloire 12*[1]

The last production series of Corsair was the F4U-7 for the French Aéronautique navale. After prototype testing, 94 F4U-7s were built and delivered in 1952–53, all manufactured at Vought's Grand Prairie, Texas, plant. (Northrop Grumman Corporation and Smithsonian Air and Space Museum)

IN THE AÉRONAUTIQUE NAVALE

HMS *Colossus* and her No. 1846 Squadron of Corsair IVs arrived at Sydney, Australia, in August 1945, too late for combat in World War II. The squadron would fly their Corsairs as top cover over prisoner of war repatriation stops on the way home but upon arrival at Royal Naval Air Station Gosport near Portsmouth would be disbanded. Incredibly, the squadron's recent-production low-time Corsair IVs—and those of the other FAA Corsair-equipped squadrons—would be either pushed over the side to settle in underwater heaps or broken up for scrap once flown ashore. The irony here is that *Colossus* would steam beyond the postwar drawdown, into the 1950s, and would again fly Corsairs from her flight decks but in French colors as units of the Aéronautique navale.

At the end of World War II, the French navy was moribund, and France's large combatant shipbuilding capability had been decimated. Reasserting her dominion over prewar colonial holdings would be difficult without the means to deliver air power on-scene when needed most to push back local insurgencies or communist-inspired rebellions. Britain and the United States recognized France's dilemma and put in motion a "loan" arrangement for surplus aircraft carriers. At variance from the terms of lend-lease before and during the war, the Mutual Defense Assistance Plan encouraged the transfer of military capital equipment without the expectation of monetary repayment but rather of "consideration" from the receiving country for end use in support of a liberalized, Western-backed international order.[2]

From Britain, the *Avenger*-class CVE HMS *Biter* became in French service the *Dixmude*, USS *Belleau Wood* and USS *Langley*, both *Independence*-class CVLs from U.S. Navy surplus became *Bois Belleau* and *La Fayette*, respectively, and from Britain, HMS *Colossus*, in a class slightly larger than the U.S. *Independence*-class CVLs, became *Arromanche*. The French would use *Dixmude* primarily for ferrying aircraft. The other three aircraft carriers hosted flight operations, with *Arromanche* routinely hosting deployments of Aéronavale squadrons. Initially, these squadrons were composed of U.S. Navy surplus SB2Cs and F6Fs for close air support. But the French desired an aircraft better suited to their carrier operations that was optimized for fighter and bomber capability. The Corsair fit the purpose but would need tailoring to French requirements.

With funds appropriated under the Military Assistance Program, pursuant to the goals of the Mutual Defense Assistance Plan, the U.S. Navy placed the order on behalf of the French for a new series of Corsair, a design tailored to the needs of the Aéronavale to be called the F4U-7. The F4U-7 was the last Corsair to be accorded its own series designation and the first Corsair series to be wholly manufactured at Vought's new factory home in Grand Prairie, Texas. The first of 94 aircraft ordered for the French made its first flight in July 1952. It was a "blended" configuration, designed around the F4U-4's R-2800–18W engine but using what essentially was the AU-1 airframe strengthened for ground attack. To the new series was added French instrumentation and pylons adapted to carry French-specific armament including the SS.11, a wire-guided anti-tank missile, and the Matra 116G, a 2.7-inch rocket clustered in pods of 18 or more rockets. Transition training for the first cohort of Aéronavale pilots was conducted by the U.S. Navy beginning in October 1952 at Naval Air Station Norfolk, Virginia.

French squadron Flottille 14.F was the first to be assigned the F4U-7 at their base in Tunisia, a French protectorate from an earlier colonial era. However the squadron's pilots had not yet received their Corsairs when they deployed for operations off Indochina. Stepping in to fill the gap, the United States hastily ferried to the French 25 well-used AU-1s from Marine Corps inventory aboard USS *Saipan* to Tourane, later known more commonly as Da Nang. The squadron would lose six of the AU-1s to ground fire from Viet Minh forces surrounding Dien Bien Phu before it fell to communist forces. Interdiction support continued even after the fall of Dien Bien Phu with strikes in other parts of Indochina from 12.F flying from *Arromanche*, then 15.F from *La Fayette*. At the end of Indochina operations, the Aéronavale had received 69 AU-1s on a direct transfer basis and returned the remaining aircraft to the United States in the Philippines.

Flottilles 14.F, 12.F, 15.F, and 17.F all flew at various times in the mid-1950s through the early 1960s from the decks of *Arromanche* and *La Fayette*. Flottilles 12.F, 14.F, and 17.F were in combat with their F4U-7s in the Algerian war, mainly from their fixed base at Bizerte, Tunisia, but occasionally from the flight deck of *Bois Belleau* when *Arromanche* and *La Fayette* were unavailable. In 1956 14.F and 15.F flew from

Arromanche and *La Fayette* in strikes on airfields around Cairo, Egypt, as France involved itself in the Suez crisis. Finally, 12.F and 17.F were used in combat to suppress rebellion in Tunisia, flying from Bizerte.

Corsairs flew on in Aéronavale livery well into the 1960s. By 1964 12.F and 14.F retired their F4U-7s to be replaced by another Vought product, the F8U Crusader. Flottilles 15.F and 17.F transitioned from Corsairs to French-designed and -manufactured Etendards.

IN THE AMERICAS

The Military Assistance Program by which the Corsair lived on as a carrier-based fighter-bomber for the Aéronavale was the transfer mechanism by which Corsairs began populating South American air forces as well. Of the three South American operators of Corsairs, only Argentina had the wherewithal to operate an aircraft carrier, the former HMS *Warrior* renamed the ARA *Independencia*. From the same *Colossus* class as the French *Arromanche*, *Independencia* benefited in Argentinian service from the installation of an angled flight deck that was a hallmark of many mid-1950 aircraft carrier modernization programs. Argentina's Corsair operations began with the transfer of 10 night-fighters, F4U-5Ns and F4U-5NLs, augmented within a year by 16 more F4U-5s and -5NLs. From their inventory of 26 aircraft, as many as half were used as spare parts machines to keep the other half flying. Those in flying condition began operating from *Independencia* as a single squadron in 1959. After seven years of carrier operations, Argentina's Corsair squadron was disbanded and the aircraft relegated to training new aviators.

Honduras was also a recipient of Corsairs as transfers from U.S. inventory. It sought more low-time F4U-5Ns and -5NLs, but most of the serviceable night-fighter versions had already been spoken for by Argentina. Honduras settled for ten night-fighter–configured aircraft but had to augment that number with the addition of nine F4U-4s that had seen much more wartime usage in U.S. squadrons.

The last South American nation to avail itself of the Military Assistance Program by taking former U.S. Corsairs was El Salvador. By 1957, very few night-fighter versions remained that had not been already transferred, and the transfer consisted mostly of older FG-1Ds. To the FG-1Ds the Salvadorans added a few more F4U-4s, but cannibalization for spare parts kept most aircraft grounded.

The last aerial combat for the Corsair occurred in an action between Honduras and El Salvador and, in a paradoxical twist, the two countries would fly their Corsairs against each other. Friction between the two was the product of a simmering cultural and social discord that flashed into armed warfare in 1969, brought to culmination by sports rivalry in the World Cup soccer matches. In the air battles that resulted, a flight of Honduran F4U-5Ns took down two El Salvador FG-1Ds. Fortunately, the Organization of American States stepped in to broker a peace settlement within days, and further armed engagement was prevented.

IN REMEMBRANCE

By some accounts there are more than 25 airworthy Corsairs privately owned or corporately sponsored in the United States, with another halfdozen operated internationally. Some can be seen regularly in airshows flying mock engagements against other replica aircraft. Some have appeared as the backdrop in weekly television fare. By far, the most authentic attempt at portraying the plane and a most poignant human moment attached to the Corsair was in the motion picture *Devotion*. The movie retells the story of Ensign Jesse Brown and his wingman, Lieutenant (junior grade) Tom

Ensign Jesse Brown is pictured on the flight deck of USS *Leyte* (CV-32) while a member of VF-32. (NARA)

USS *Leyte* (CV-32), moored off Yokosuka, prepares to get underway on 1 December 1950 for operations off Korea. VF-32 F4U-4s are parked in front of *Leyte*'s island. Three days later, the squadron would lose two Corsairs when Ensign Jesse Brown was downed by gunfire and Lieutenant (junior grade) Tom Hudner crash-landed his Corsair next to Brown's in an attempt to free him from the wreckage. (NHHC)

Hudner, and their comradeship while flying F4U-4s in VF-32 from USS *Leyte* (CV-32) in the Korean War. The story carries added emotional impact for its portrayal of Brown's experiences as the first African American naval aviator and the taunting he overcame to become a valued squadron member.

With the film's nationwide release, many people at least several generations removed from that era learned for the first time of Brown's heroism and tragic death in his Corsair, and of Hudner's courageous but unsuccessful attempt to rescue Brown. The two were part of a six-plane formation that launched on 4 December 1950 to provide air support to Marine infantry at risk of being overwhelmed by Communist Chinese forces at the Chosin Reservoir. Enemy ground fire damaged Brown's plane, forcing him to put his Corsair down on a small open patch of snow-covered ground at the base of steep mountain slopes. The crash-landing pinned Brown in the cockpit, miles behind enemy lines. When Brown did not respond to radio calls, Hudner intentionally crash-landed his Corsair next to Brown's to render aid and extract him from the burning aircraft. A rescue helicopter arrived and its pilot assisted Hudner, but was not successful in extracting Brown. As darkness closed in, Hudner was forced to leave in the rescue helicopter. Brown, unconscious, remained trapped in his Corsair and expired from his wounds and the cold.

To enhance the film's realism, producers sought airworthy examples of Corsairs. Key scenes included an F4U-7, F4U-1, FG-1D, and the only model truly accurate to the event, an F4U-4. Flying scenes were done near Savannah, Georgia, and for winter-like weather, near Pasco, Washington.[3] The restored Corsairs in the film help evoke a long-ago war that is little remembered today but one in which the Corsair played an outsize role. As historian Peter Mersky put it; "The value of the Chance Vought F4U Corsair cannot be overestimated. Rugged and powerful, the dependable Corsair was in constant action, from sea and land forces. It was viewed with real affection by the men on the ground."[4]

NOTES

1. Patrick Marchand and Junko Takamori, *Les Ailes de Gloire 12* (Paris: Editions d'Along, 2003).

2. Caroline Lichtenberg, "The Mutual Defense Assistance Program," Federal Reserve System Board of Governors, 26 September 1950, https://www.federalreserve.gov/pubs/rfd/1950/148/rfd148.pdf.

3. Jan Tegler, "Flying for 'Devotion,'" *Flight Journal*, March 2023, https://www.flightjournal.com/flying-devotion-behind-scenes-pilots-brought-story-ensign-jesse-brown-lt-jg-thomas-hudner-life/.

4. Mersky, *U.S. Marine Corps Aviation since 1912*, 128.

BIBLIOGRAPHY

"Admiral C. W. Nimitz's Message to the Pacific Fleet." 2 September 1945. https://www.history.navy.mil/research/archives/digital-exhibits-highlights/vj-day/surrender/nimitz-message.html#:~:text=On%20board%20all%20naval%20vessels,1941%2C%20is%20at%20an%20end.

Anderson, W. S. "Final Report on Service Acceptance Trials of Model XF4U-1 Airplane No. 1143." Vought Aircraft Company Collection, B44/F05, History of Aviation Archives, Special Collections and Archives Division, Eugene McDermott Library, University of Texas at Dallas.

Barber, Stuart B. *Naval Aviation Combat Statistics World War II*. OPNAV-P- 23V No. A129. Washington, DC: Air Branch, Office of Naval Intelligence, Office of the Chief of Naval Operations, 17 June 1946.

"Battle of Okinawa." Intelligence Digest, Amphibious Forces, Pacific Fleet, April 1945. https://www.nationalww2museum.org/war/topics/battle-of-okinawa.

Berg, A. Scott. *Lindbergh*. New York: Berkley Books, 1999.

Blackburn, Tom. *The Jolly Rogers*. Pacifica, CA: Pacifica Press, 1997.

Booth, C. T. "Final Flight Report of Production Inspection Trials on Model F4U-1 Airplane." Flight Test, U.S. Naval Air Station Patuxent River, MD, 31 October 1944. http://www.wwiiaircraftperformance.org.

Bowman, Martin W. *The Men Who Flew the Vought F4U Corsair*. Barnsley, UK: Pen & Sword Books, 2021.

Boyington, Gregory. "VMF-214 War Diary 10/1–31/43." Record Group 38, National Archives and Records Administration, College Park, MD.

Brown, Eric. "Grumman F4F Martlet." Armoured Aircraft Carriers in World War II. https://www.armouredcarriers.com/grumman-f4f-martlet-variants.

Bureau of Aeronautics. "Class VF Airplanes—Request for Designs and Informal Proposals." Amended June 1938. Record Group 72, National Archives and Records Administration, College Park, MD.

Carrier Qualification Unit Glenview. "Action Message #1831." 5 April 1943. Record Group 38, National Archives and Records Administration, College Park, MD.

Chambers, Joseph R. *Cave of the Winds—The Remarkable History of the Langley Full-Scale Wind Tunnel*. Washington, DC: NASA, 2014. https://www.nasa.gov/sites/default/files/files/Cave_of_the_Winds_pdf.pdf.

Clark, W. E . "VF-10 War History." Record Group 38, National Archives and Records Administration, College Park, MD. https://catalog.archives.gov/id/77659151?objectPage=19.

Condon, John Pomeroy. *Corsairs and Flattops*. Annapolis, MD: Naval Institute Press, 1998.

Condon, John Pomeroy, and Peter Mersky. *Corsairs to Panthers*. Washington, DC: CreateSpace Independent Publishing, 2002.

Connors, Jack. *The Engines of Pratt & Whitney*. Reston, VA: AIAA, Inc., 2010.

D'Angina, James. *Vought F4U Corsair*. Oxford: Osprey Publishing, 2014.

Dean, Francis H., ed. *Report of Joint Fighter Conference*. Atglen, PA: Schiffer Publishing, 1998.

Duncan, Gay. "Cleland on Cleveland." *Large Scale Planes*, 2011. https://www.largescaleplanes.com/articles/article.php?aid=904.

Durgin, C. T. "Proposed Use of F4U Aircraft in Carrier Air Groups." 28 June 1944. http://www.researcheratlarge.com/Aircraft/F4U/F4UCarrierSuitability.html.

Egan, Charles E. "Expert to Survey Brewster's Plant." *New York Times*, 1 June 1944.

Francillon, René J. *Grumman Aircraft*. Annapolis, MD: Naval Institute Press, 1989.

Gamble, Bruce. *Black Sheep One*. New York: Random House, 2000.

Gandt, Robert. *The Twilight Warriors*. New York: Crown Publishing, 2010.

Graff, Cory. "How the Navy Tamed the 'Killer Corsair.'" *Smithsonian Magazine*, June 2021. https://www.smithsonianmag.com/air-space-magazine/spoiler-alert-1-180977803/.

Gray, Robert Hampton. "Member Profile." Canada's Aviation Hall of Fame, 1974. https://cahf.ca/robert-hampton-gray/.

Guyton, Boone. *Whistling Death*. Atglen, PA: Schiffer Publishing, 1994.

Hill, R. E. "CAG 84 Action Reports." 27 May 1945. Record Group 38, National Archives and Records Administration, College Park, MD.

Kinzey, Bert. *F4U Corsair in Detail & Scale, Part 1: XF4U through F2G*. Carrollton, TX: Squadron/Signal, 1998.

———. *F4U Corsair in Detail & Scale, Part 2: F4U-4 through F4U-7*. Carrollton, TX: Squadron/Signal, 1998.

Knapp, Lew. "Corsair." *Sikorsky Archives News*, March 2001. https://sikorskyarchives.com/wp-content/uploads/archives-newsletters/NEWS-2001-03.pdf.

Lanham, H. P. "Operations Report, Ser. 059-50." 2 August 1950. http://www.koreanwar-educator.org/topics/Reports/after_action/korean_combat_action_reports_for_carrier_air_group_5.pdf.

Larson, George C. "The Wasp Engine's Great Leap Forward." *Smithsonian Magazine*, December 2017. https://www.smithsonianmag.com/air-space-magazine/why-the-wasp-is-wonderful-180967115/.

Lerch, Alfred. "Voices from the Fleet." Recorded interview, ca. 1945. Intrepid Sea, Air, and Space Museum.

Lichtenberg, Caroline. "The Mutual Defense Assistance Program." Federal Reserve System Board of Governors, 26 September 1950. https://www.federalreserve.gov/pubs/rfd/1950/148/rfd148.pdf.

Lindbergh, Charles A. *The Wartime Journals of Charles A. Lindbergh*. New York: Harcourt Brace Jovanovich, 1970.

Lundstrom, John. *The First Team*. Annapolis, MD: Naval Institute Press, 1984.

———. *The First Team and the Guadalcanal Campaign*. Annapolis, MD: Naval Institute Press, 1994.

Macdonald, Rod. *Task Force 58*. Annapolis, MD: Naval Institute Press, 2021.

Marchand, Patrick, and Junko Takamori. *Les Ailes de Gloire 12*. Paris: Editions d'Along, 2003.

McCutcheon, Kimble D. "Pratt & Whitney Double Wasp (R-2800)." Aircraft Engine Historical Society, 10 March 2002. https://www.enginehistory.org/Piston/P&W/R-2800/r-2800.shtml.

Megee, Vernon. "Evolution of Marine Aviation." Oral History Transcript. Washington, DC: Historical Division, U.S. Marine Corps, 1973.

Mersky, Peter B. *The Grim Reapers: Fighting Squadron 10 in WWII*. Mesa, AZ: Champlin Museum Press, 1986.

———. *U.S. Marine Corps Aviation since 1912*. Annapolis, MD: Naval Institute Press, 2009.

Meyer, Corky. "Hellcat versus Corsair—Grumman Test Pilot Flies the Competition." 17 November 2020. https://www.pressreader.com/usa/wwii-fighters/20201117/281603833007728.

Millington, William A. "VMF-124 Combat Report." https://airgroup4.com/marines.htm.

Montgomery, Robert E. *Pacific Corsair*. Wellington, NZ: Venture Publications, 2023.

Moore, Stephen L. *Rain of Steel*. Annapolis, MD: Naval Institute Press, 2020.

Morgan, Thomas. "The Industrial Mobilization of World War II." *Army History Magazine*, no. 30, Spring 1994.

Morison, Samuel Eliot. *History of United States Naval Operations in World War II*, vol. XIV, *Victory in the Pacific*. Boston: Little, Brown, 1968.

Nimitz, Chester. "Message to Pacific Fleet, September 2, 1945." Naval History and Heritage Command. https://www.history.navy.mil/research/archives/digital-exhibits-highlights/vj-day/surrender/nimitz-message.html.

Odell, William C. "The Development of Night Fighters in World War II." *Naval History Magazine* 3, no. 1, January 1989. https://www.usni.org/magazines/naval-history-magazine/1989/january/development-night-fighters-world-war-ii.

Okumiya, Masatake, and Jiro Horikoshi. *Zero*. New York: E. P. Dutton, 1956.

Peattie, Mark R. *Sunburst*. Annapolis, MD: Naval Institute Press, 2001.

Penland, Dane. "Vought F4U-1D Corsair." Smithsonian National Air and Space Museum, Steven F. Udvar-Hazy Center, Chantilly, VA. https://airandspace.si.edu/collection-objects/vought-f4u-1d-corsair/nasm_A19610124000.

Pennsylvania Bureau for Historic Preservation. "Johnsville Naval Air Development Center History." https://explorepahistory.com/hmarker.php?markerId=1-A-2F4.

Popham, Hugh. "The British Eastern Fleet." Armoured Aircraft Carriers of World War II. https://www.armouredcarriers.com/british-eastern-fleet-royal-navy-operations-in-the-indian-ocean.

Ramsay, Annetta. "Landmarks and Legacies: Hal Jackson Helped Sink Yamato." *Denton* (TX) *Record-Chronicle*, March 15, 2020. https://dentonrc.com/news/landmarks-legacies-hal-jackson-helped-sink-yamato-the-largest-battleship-ever/article_9de56055-6853-57d0-b675-84491b93de57.html.

Ramsey, Paul H. "Memorandum for the VF Design Desk." NA83-FT-44016, May 1944. National Archives and Records Administration, College Park, MD.

Reynolds, Clark G. *Admiral John Towers*. Annapolis, MD: Naval Institute Press, 1991.

———. *The Fast Carriers*. Annapolis, MD: Naval Institute Press, 1992.

Rezich, Nick. "The 1947 Cleveland Air Races." *Vintage Airplane* 33, no. 7, 2005.

Rielly, Robin L. *Kamikazes, Corsairs, and Picket Ships*. Havertown, PA: Casemate Press, 2008.

Sakaida, Henry. *Imperial Japanese Navy Aces 1937–1945*. Oxford: Osprey Publishing, 1999.

Sherrod, Robert. *History of Marine Corps Aviation in World War II*. Washington, DC: Combat Forces Press, 1952.

Sibila, Alfred I. "Designing the Bent-Wing Bird." *Naval History Magazine* 9, no. 1, February 1995. https://www.usni.org/magazines/naval-history-magazine/1995/february/designing-bent-wing-bird.

Singer, Bayla. "Engineering Success: Pratt & Whitney Aircraft, 1925–1940." *Business and Economic History* 27, no. 1, 1998. http://www.jstor.org/stable/23703077.

"Sweetheart of Okinawa: Kadena's Corsair Squadrons." 18th Wing History Office, Kadena Air Base News, 10 April 2013. https://www.kadena.af.mil/News/Article/417286/the-sweetheart-of-okinawa-kadenas-corsair-squadrons/.

Tegler, Jan. "Flying for 'Devotion.'" *Flight Journal*, 24 March 2023. https://www.flightjournal.com/flying-devotion-behind-scenes-pilots-brought-story-ensign-jesse-brown-ltjg-thomas-hudner-life/.

Thomason, Tommy H. *Bell XFL-1 Airabonita*. Simi Valley, CA: Steve Ginter, 2008.

———. "Vought XF4U-1 Corsair." Tailhook Topics, 4 September 2013. http://tailspintopics.blogspot.com/2013/09/vought-xf4u-1-corsair.html.

———. *F4U Units of the Korean War*. Oxford: Osprey Publishing, 2012.

Thompson, Warren. *Naval Aviation in the Korean War*. Barnsley, UK: Pen & Sword Aviation, 2012.

Tillman, Barrett. *Corsair*. Annapolis, MD: Naval Institute Press, 1979.

———. *U.S. Marine Corps Fighter Squadrons of World War II*. Oxford: Osprey Publishing, 2014.

Towers, John H. "Action Message #180022." 19 August 1943. Record Group 38, National Archives and Records Administration, College Park, MD.

Trapnell, Frederick M. Jr., and Dana Trapnell Tibbitts. *Harnessing the Sky*. Annapolis, MD: Naval Institute Press, 2015.

Tuttle, M. H. "Combat Evaluation of Zeke 52 with F4U-1D." Technical Air Intelligence Center, NAS Anacostia, November 1944. http://www.wwiiaircraftperformance.org.

"U.S. Ship Force Levels." Naval History and Heritage Command. https://www.history.navy.mil/resesarch/histories/ship-histories/us-ship-force-levels.html.

"VMF-314 Aircraft Action Report." 3 June 1945. Record Group 38, National Archives and Records Administration, College Park, MD.

"VMF(CV)-211 War Diary." 1–30 April 1945. Record Group 38, National Archives and Records Administration, College Park, MD.

Walsh, Kenneth. "U.S. Marine Aviation in World War II: VMF-124 in the Solomons." Interview by Jeffrey Kwallek. Research Report 88-1515. Maxwell Air Force Base, AL: Air Command and Staff College. https://apps.dtic.mil/sti/pdfs/ADA192519.pdf.

Whitby, Michael. "Navy Blue Fighter Pilot." Vintage Wings of Canada. https://tomato-hibiscus-5kcf.squarespace.com/stories/donsheppardepisode2.

White, Graham. *R-2800: Pratt & Whitney's Dependable Masterpiece*. Warrendale, PA: SAE, 2001.

Wilson, E. E. "Biographies." Vought Heritage. 22 January 1931. https://www.vought.org/peoplaces/html/bcmveew.html.

Young, Edward. *F4F Wildcat vs. A6M Zeke-sen*. Oxford: Osprey Publishing, 2013.

THE VOUGHT F4U-1D CORSAIR AT THE SMITHSONIAN NATIONAL AIR AND SPACE MUSEUM

The Smithsonian National Air and Space Museum restored Vought F4U-1D Corsair, wings unfolded, on the ground outside Building 20 at the NASM Paul E. Garber Facility, Suitland, Maryland, on October 14, 1980. (Dale E. Hrabak, Smithsonian National Air and Space Museum)

On the night of January 27, 1981, Vought F4U-1D BuNo. 50375 rolled through the doors of the Smithsonian National Air and Space Museum after a multi-year effort involving research, disassembly, cleaning, and restoration. The airframe experienced years of service with the U.S. Navy, which became obvious during the restoration efforts as corrosion and dents were found and fixed. The finished aircraft, now hanging at the museum's Steven F. Udvar-Hazy Center, highlights the important role the Corsair played in the Second World War, and honors the brave men who flew it.

Corsair #50375 was delivered to the Navy by Vought on April 26, 1944. It is not known where it was originally delivered, but by October 1944 it was assigned to the VF-10, the infamous "Grim Reapers" of the USS *Enterprise*. A month or so later found #50735 with VF-89 as it was being equipped at Naval Air Station Atlantic City. The airframe travelled with the squadron to both Naval Air Station Oceana and Naval Air Station Norfolk. On June 30, 1945, it was moved to Quantico Marine Air Station to join other surplus aircraft as the need for them dissipated as the war was coming to an end. Following the war, the airframe was assigned to locations such as Naval Air Station Memphis, as well as the Naval Air Technical Training Center at Pensacola, Florida. #50375 was finally stricken from the official operational records of the U.S. Navy on April 30, 1946, after which it was sent to the Naval Air Technical Training Center in Norman, Oklahoma. It remained in Norman, Oklahoma until November 21, 1955, when it was shipped back to Norfolk " . . . for reconditioning and canned storage pending readiness of the NAM [the National Air Museum, the name of the National Air and Space Museum before space flight was added]." The airframe was most likely used to train future U.S. Navy aircraft mechanics at the Technical Training Centers during its final years of service, offering an excellent hands-on platform for aspiring students. The museum uncovered signs of this type of service as it was prepared for its display debut.

Aircraft that arrive at the National Air and Space Museum often show signs of their service life, whether that be patches covering flak damage from bombing missions or scrapes in the paint and misaligned panels from years of flight. #50375 revealed signs of its time at the technical schools as the plane was disassembled and the paint was removed to treat corrosion. The fin of the aircraft was found to have the bureau number 57101 on it, while the right elevator and stabilizer were numbered 50522. It is most likely that these parts of the aircraft were swapped with others some time earlier, most likely by the aircraft mechanics being trained to do such things in a combat situation at some future forward operating base. The fabric surfaces of the aircraft were also replaced at this time and were painted and doped in the same manner as the originals. All the parts of the aircraft were photographically documented, disassembled, cleaned, preserved, and reassembled to ensure the aircraft would last for generations as it was displayed in the museum.

At this point in the process, it was decided to repaint the aircraft in the style of Corsairs that had seen combat experience in the skies above the Pacific. Curators conducted a search for original photographs identifying markings so the paint job could be as authentic as possible. A photograph was located of ship #56, operating with VMF-113 over Eniwetok on July 9, 1944. Marine Fighter Squadron VMF-113, known as the "Whistling Devils," had served throughout the war in the Pacific, and offered an excellent example of the type of unit that effectively used the Corsair in combat. The decision to paint the museum's aircraft #50375 as a Marine Corps squadron Corsair also allowed for an interesting interaction once the restoration was completed.

It took 9,315 hours to take Corsair #50375 from how it was received from the Navy to the plane that is currently on display in the museum. In October 1980,

Smithsonian National Air and Space Museum employee Bob Padgett at work on the restoration of the Vought F4U-1D Corsair in Building 10 of the NASM Paul E. Garber Facility in Suitland, Maryland, April 17, 1980. (Dale E. Hrabak, Smithsonian National Air and Space Museum)

VMF-214
WAR DIARY

(opposite page, clockwise from the top) Smithsonian National Air and Space Museum restoration specialist Charles "Charlie" Parmley (left) speaks with World War II US Marine Corps ace Major Gregory W. "Pappy" Boyington USMC (Ret.) (right) in front of the propeller of Vought F4U-1D Corsair outside Building 10 of the NASM Garber Facility during a visit by Boyington with members of Marine Fighter Squadron 214 "Black Sheep" to view the restored aircraft on October 6, 1980. (Smithsonian National Air and Space Museum)

World War II US Marine Corps ace Major Gregory W. "Pappy" Boyington USMC (Ret.) sits in the cockpit of Vought F4U-1D outside Building 10 of the Smithsonian National Air and Space Museum Garber Facility during a visit with members of Marine Fighter Squadron 214 "Black Sheep" to view the restored aircraft on October 6, 1980. (Smithsonian National Air and Space Museum)

Retired World War II US Marine Corps ace Major Gregory W. "Pappy" Boyington (front row, second from right) poses with members of Marine Fighter Squadron 214 "Black Sheep" in front of Vought F4U-1D Corsair outside Building 10 of the Smithsonian National Air and Space Museum Garber Facility during a visit to view the NASM-restored aircraft on October 6, 1980. (Smithsonian National Air and Space Museum)

as the museum was placing the final touches on the Corsair, surviving veterans from Marine Corps Fighter Squadron 214 visited the aircraft at the Smithsonian National Air and Space Museum's Garber Facility in Suitland, Maryland. The squadron is known better as the "Black Sheep" squadron, and its commander Major Gregory "Pappy" Boyington was on hand to see #50375 in its new paint scheme. Major Boyington discussed the qualities of the Corsair with museum staff, posed for pictures both inside and outside of the aircraft, and even took time to sign the rear wall inside the right wheel well of the aircraft.

Vought F4U-1D Corsair BuNo. 50375 is now one of the first aircraft visitors see when then arrive at the Steven F. Udvar-Hazy Center. Its distinctive gull wings and deep blue color are hard to miss. It represents not only the impact of the Corsair in the skies over numerous islands across the Pacific during World War II, but also the importance of U.S. Naval and Marine Corps aviation to our nation's history.

On the night of January 27-28, 1981, the Vought F4U Corsair was moved from the Smithsonian's aircraft restoration facility in suburban Maryland to the Air and Space Museum for installation as a display. Four views of Smithsonian National Air and Space Museum restored Vought F4U-1D Corsair being moved from the NASM Paul E. Garber Facility in Suitland, Maryland (upper left, moving out of Building 10) into the NASM Mall Building in Washington, D.C. (lower right, moving into Gallery 104). (Smithsonian National Air and Space Museum)

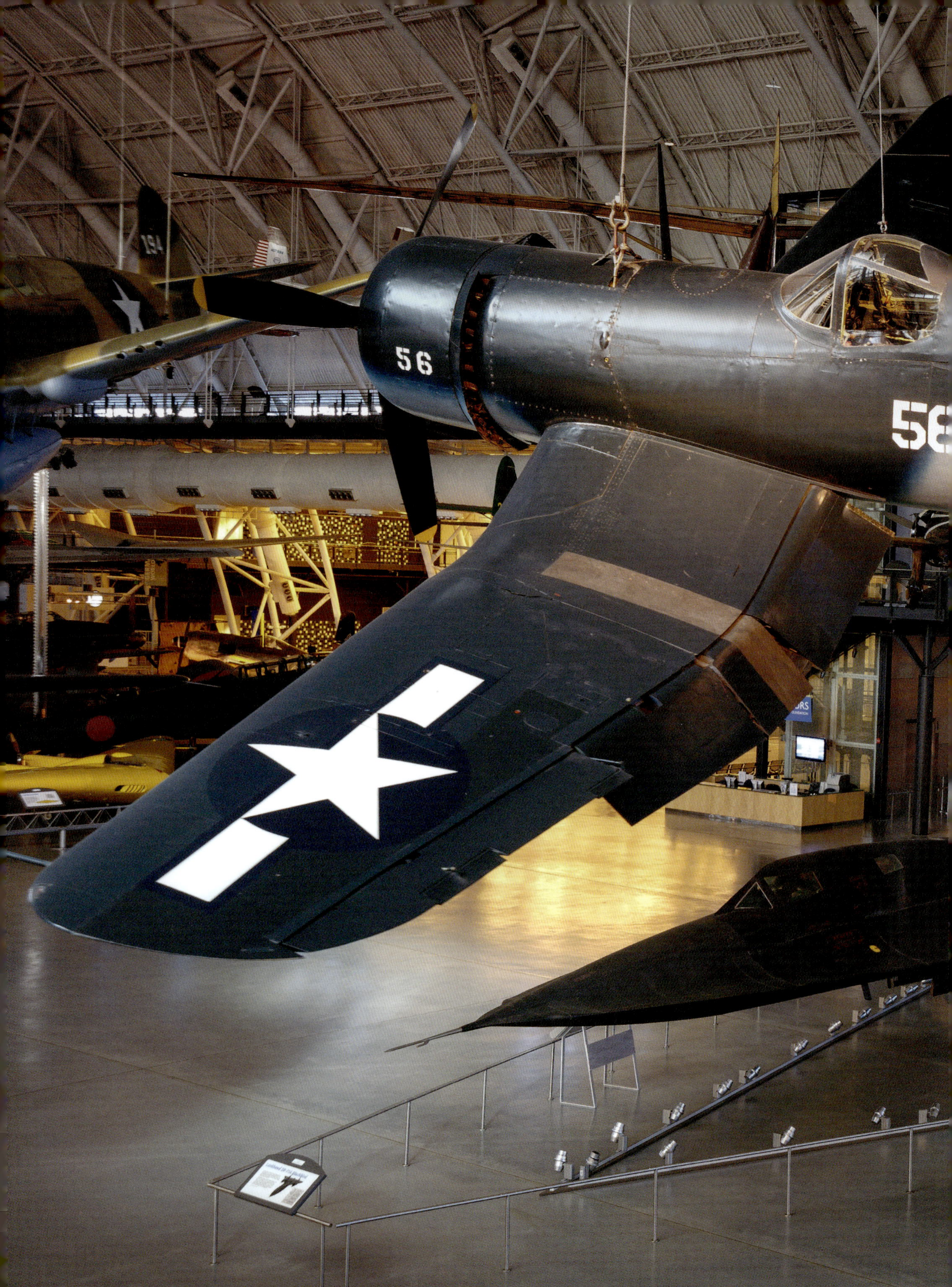
56
58

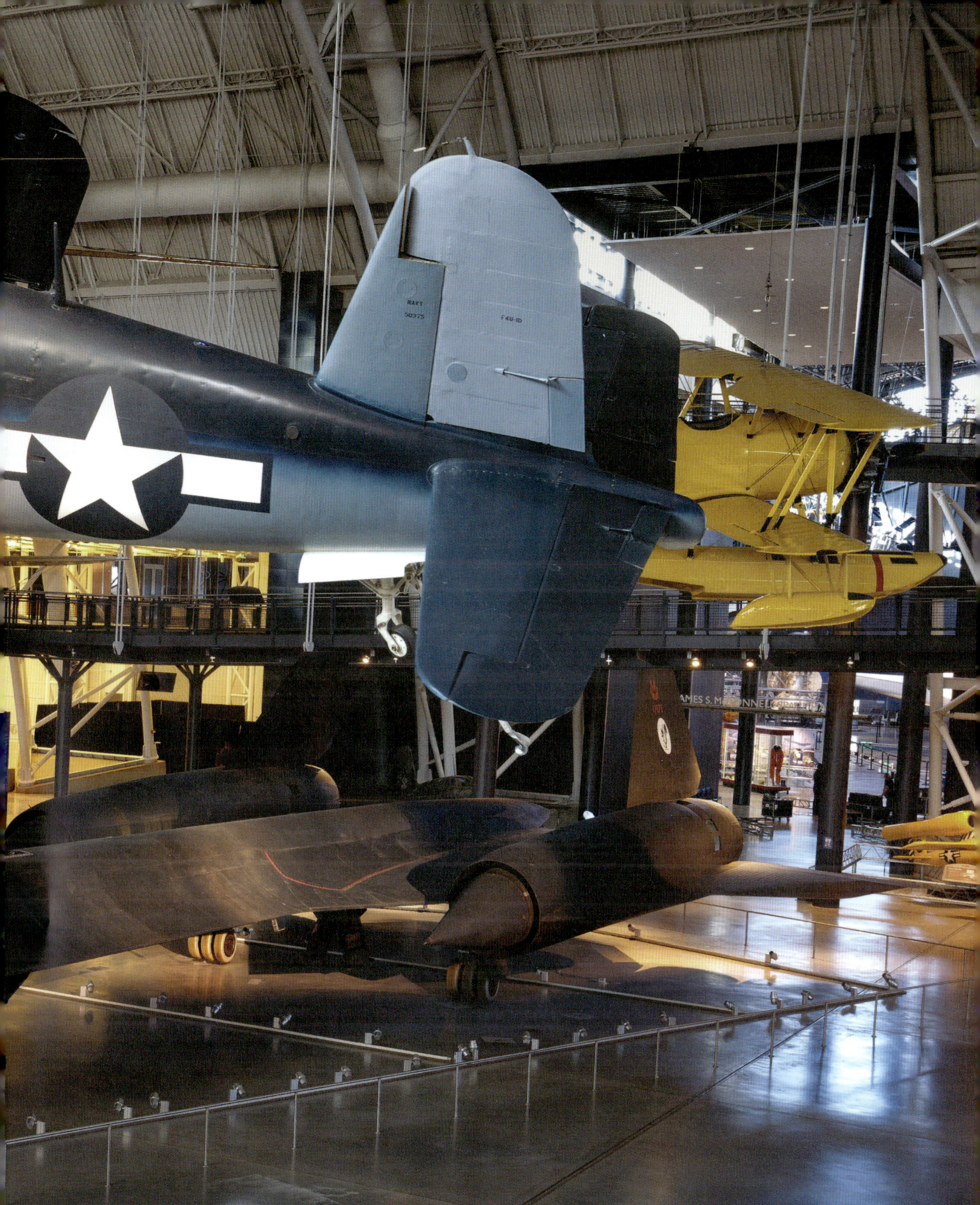

Vought F4U-1D Corsair, in the foreground, on display at the National Air and Space Museum, Steven F. Udvar-Hazy Center, Chantilly, Virginia. (Dane Penland, Smithsonian National Air and Space Museum)

World of Warships is a free-to-play, naval warfare-themed, massively multiplayer online game produced and published by Wargaming. Like their other games, *World of Tanks* (WoT) and *World of Warplanes* (WoWP), players take control of historic vehicles to battle others in player-vs-player battles or play cooperatively against bots in a player-versus-environment (PvE) mode. *World of Warships* (WoWs) was originally released for on PC in 2015 and was followed in 2018 by a mobile adaptation, *World of Warships Blitz*. The PlayStation 4 and Xbox One console version, titled *World of Warships: Legends*, released in 2019 and became available on PlayStation 5 and Xbox Series X/S in April 2021.

Developed by Wargaming d.o.o. in Belgrade, Serbia, *World of Warships* (PC) currently has millions of registered players – playing on four main servers across the globe. More than 500 dedicated staff members work on a four-week update cycle to bring new features, ships, and mechanics to the game – keeping gameplay fresh and inviting to new players. The game features more than 700 ships, spread across 13 different in-game nations. Ships are designed based on historical documents and actual blueprints from the first half of the 20th century, and it takes from two to six months on average to create each of these ships. There are more than 23 ports to choose from, and 16 of them are re-created based on historic harbors and port towns.

There are five different ship classes—destroyers, cruisers, battleships, aircraft carriers, and submarines—with each class offering a different gameplay experience. Ships are arranged in tiers between I and X, plus so-called superships, which represent the pinnacle of naval engineering from World War II and the early Cold War era. Players must progress through ship classes and tiers to reach tier X, after which they get access to these behemoths. Each warship needs a naval commander to lead it into battle, and there are many commanders to choose from in *World of Warships*, including more than 15 iconic historical figures. In *World of Warships*, players can battle on more than 40 maps. There are seven different permanent or seasonal Battle Types to choose from, including Co-op Battles, Random Battles, Ranked Battles, Clan Battles, Brawls, and Scenarios. From time to time, additional special Event battles are held.

An important component of *World of Warships*' gameplay is the management of aerial assets, and with the sheer number of aircraft carriers you can take into battle, you can be sure that the game has modeled each and every historical naval aircraft with as much detail and care as the ships themselves. The Vought F4U Corsair, for example, which was famously used the U.S. Navy in the later stages of the Pacific War and Korea, is represented in different variants aboard several ships American and even British ships in the game. In the game, Corsairs fill the role of Attack Aircraft squadrons, and can come equipped with either HVAR 127 mm unguided rockets, or the misleadingly large Tiny Tim rockets.

Developed by the team behind *World of Warships* for PC, *World of Warships: Legends* is a different entry in Wargaming's flagship nautical franchise that takes full advantage of the power and capabilities of home consoles. *World of Warships: Legends* brings the online naval action loved by millions to home consoles for the very first time, alongside a host of content and features exclusive to the console experience. *World of Warships: Legends* is now available to download from the PlayStation® Store and Microsoft Store. Players can now wage wars across a variety of maps, in numerous warships, and enjoy stunning oceanic vistas with glorious HDR support on PlayStation®4 and Xbox One X. Full 4K support is available on PlayStation®4 Pro and PlayStation®5, and Xbox One X too! and *Legends* also supports standard high-def on PlayStation®4 and Xbox One, with more intriguing graphics on the horizon.

Wargaming proudly supports various charitable causes that members of the gaming and history community deeply care for:

Supporting veterans and servicemembers

- Operation Lifeboat (2020) raised $150,000 USD for Stack Up's mental health awareness helpline
- Remembrance charity drive (2020) raised $45,000 USD for Help for Heroes, which supports UK veterans and service members
- Project Valor (2017) saw *WoWS*, *WoT*, and *WoWP* raising $75,000 USD for a veteran housing program

DISTINGUISHED FLYING CROSS

The Distinguished Flying Cross was established in 1926. Since then, it has been awarded for heroism and outstanding achievements demonstrated during an air battle. U.S. service members, foreign military, and even civil aviators can receive the cross. David McCampbell, the highest scoring ace of World War II, received, among many other awards, three Distinguished Flying Crosses.

During the Pacific Campaign, under McCampbell's command, Carrier Air Group 15, aboard the aircraft carrier *Essex* (CV-9), destroyed more enemy aircraft and ships than any other U.S. Navy squadron.

CUT!

Aircraft arrived on a carrier from the stern of the ship, and the pilots usually approached from the port side. Hence, the platform specifically designated for the signaling officers was situated on the port side of the ship—at the rear part of the deck.

If the landing was going well, and the pilot followed all the instructions of the LSO (landing signal officer), the latter gave the final signal allowing the pilot to land. Officially it was called the Cut Throttle signal—which stemmed from the "cutthroat" gesture made by the signal officer.

Preserving historical ship museums

World of Warships partners with museums across the world to support the preservation of naval history and the education of the global community.

In celebration of 2021's International Museum Day, Wargaming, in partnership with Verizon, organized The Longest Night of Museums livestream. The online event included free virtual tours of 15 different naval museums worldwide, attracting million viewers on Twitch alone.

In July 2021 Wargaming partnered with Imperial War Museum to launch an interactive gaming room atop London's iconic museum ship HMS *Belfast*.

- $50,000 USD raised for the restoration of USS *Batfish, Muskogee* (2019)
- $400,000 USD raised for the restoration of USS *Texas, Houston* (since 2017)
- $20,000 USD raised in partnership with the French-speaking community for the restoration of the submarine *Espadon* (2021)
- $50,000 USD raised for the Nauticus museum to restore one of the main turrets of USS *Wisconsin*. (2024)

Supporting local communities

In two 24-hour charity livestreams $43,000 USD (2019) and $130,000 USD (2021) were raised for Save the Children organization.

- $78,000 USD raised for Team Rubicon and the victims of Hurricane Harvey in 2017
- $106,000 USD raised with *WoT* and *WoT*:MA for the Hawai'i Community Foundation Maui's Strong Fund in September 2023